Case Studies in Industrial Relations

G D Green

Pitman

PITMAN PUBLISHING
128 Long Acre, London WC2E 9AN

© G. D. Green 1988

First published in Great Britain 1988

British Library Cataloguing in Publication Data
Green, G. D. (Geoffrey David), *1948–*
   Case studies in industrial relations.
   1. Industrial relations – Case studies
   331'.0722

ISBN 0 273 02551 1

Printed in Great Britain at The Bath Press, Avon

Contents

Preface   *vii*
Acknowledgements   *ix*
Introduction   *xi*
Brief summary of cases   *xvi*
Table of topics covered   *xxiii*

Case 1   The annual wage negotiations   1
Case 2   Growing pains   11
Case 3   Defective procedures are harmful   20
Case 4   Sorry, you're redundant   27
Case 5   Going to arbitration   31
Case 6   Technology agreement   37
Case 7   Union membership agreement   41
Case 8   Disciplinary procedure   45
Case 9   Catering for the workers   49
Case 10   Breaking the mould   54
Case 11   The mushrooming problem   63
Case 12   Custom and practice   72
Case 13   The high-risk driver   76
Case 14   Temper! Temper!   82
Case 15   Strangers at work   88
Case 16   The unsuitable shop steward   93
Case 17   The shop floor worker   100
Case 18   Drunk and disorderly   105
Case 19   The Skittles player   109
Case 20   Redundancy at Toolcraft   112

Appendix   Learning points   116

Preface

This book is essentially written as source material for those studying industrial relations, to apply what they know about industrial relations to novel situations, to gain further insights into the subject and to practise essential skills. By doing, we learn, and this is particularly true in using case studies, especially in a subject that is so practical.

The additional virtue of case studies is that they provide a realistic means of practising and improving skills. Industrial relations is a subject that requires a balance of knowledge and skills. The more that these can be tried and tested in a training situation, the more the student will develop before applying what has been learnt in a real situation at work.

The book provides twenty cases of varying length and type. I have tried to cover a range of situations in a diversity of sectors to give variety. The subjects covered include all the main areas of industrial relations and a table is included which shows the range of topics covered; this can be used to choose a relevant case for a particular purpose. The cases all include an introduction to the topics covered and a guide is given on what previous learning activities the student should have undertaken. The possession of such previous knowledge and skills is not essential but the topics listed provide an indication of what is helpful in dealing with the case.

The cases are written in a range of styles, some descriptive, others containing narrative. Some focus on a particular issue, others cover a broader spectrum of the organisation. The majority of the cases are based on some real, live situation. I have culled the ideas and information from my own industrial experience, my contact with firms while I have been in education, from tribunal cases, official reports (such as from ACAS) and anecdotes related by people I have met, which have triggered off an idea.

All the cases end with a range of exercises. These are designed to focus on a range of activities that can be used by students and tutors. Clearly, these can be amended or new ones included to suit the needs of a particular group of students. The exercises include some for the individual student who is working alone (e.g. on a distance/open learning based course) or is given the exercise at the end of a class activity. Several exercises are group-based activities. The nature of industrial relations lends itself to this type of activity. These are vital for the development of the skills required of industrial relations practitioners. The development of skills is also in tune with current developments in education and training where much emphasis is being laid on the acquisition, development and assessment of skills, for example on BTEC courses.

The cases tend to be longer cases rather than 'case-ettes'. This is deliberate. There are already a number of sources of smaller, single topic cases and if one cannot be found a tutor could easily write one. Longer cases are useful for taking an in-depth and comprehensive look at a situation and they can ideally be used as problem-solving activities. I have also tended to steer away from too many cases based on tribunal hearings, particularly unfair dismissal cases. Again, there is much source material available in this area and tutors can access tribunal reports and use them instructively on their courses.

It would be useful that, where a case requires some definite, factual knowledge, such as legal requirements or points from an official Code of Practice, the students are given the opportunity of acquiring this before the case commences. It is wasteful to spend time arguing about facts that could have been established beforehand; this would aid the smooth running of a case if the information were made available beforehand, in the form of a handout or booklet, to enable students to make use of it as reference material during the case.

The book can be used by students on a range of courses, both qualification-based and shorter courses or seminars used for a specific training purpose. The cases can be adapted for use by a range of students. They are suitable for Business Studies students on BTEC courses (National and Higher National), Management Studies students, such as NEBSS, ISM, IIM, CMS and DMS courses and post-experience courses, such as the BTEC Continuing Education Units. Training courses covering particular aspects of industrial relations should be able to utilise some of the cases.

Acknowledgements

I wish to thank all those who have helped in the compilation of the cases. Many people have contributed unknowingly; those I have worked for and with in the past, students in class as they relate incidents at their place of work, managers as I visit them, colleagues at work, friends in conversation; they have all contributed to the fund of knowledge that hopefully is apparent in the cases. I have clearly adapted the information to protect anonymity and to bring out certain aspects of a case. Often I have transposed a situation from one industry to another to add to the variety of situations covered by the cases.

I thank my publisher and their reviewers who came up with many useful criticisms and suggestions while the book was being written. Finally, and not least, I thank my family for the great forebearance they have shown while dad was locked away, glued to the screen of a word processor or buried in drafts and corrections. They have been patient, understanding and most supportive, encouraging me to keep going when I sometimes felt otherwise. Any faults with the book are entirely my responsibility. I hope that you will find the cases stimulating and an enjoyable learning experience in a very interesting subject area.

Introduction

Defining a case study

There are a number of definitions of what a case study is. The following is a useful working definition: 'a teaching device that utilises real life situations by placing students in a realistic position, presents them with actual conditions, forces them to think analytically and constructively, makes them consider alternatives, and forces them to arrive at a decision they can substantiate'. The primary purpose of a case study is to apply knowledge, skills, techniques, concepts and principles to situations that accord with reality. They require active student participation which is based on the sound educational principle that students are more likely to learn when they are involved and not merely passive observers. Hence the moves in vocational education to student-centred learning.

A further basic point about a case study is that it is integrative in nature. Again, this accords with reality as the practice of management utilises a range of topics in dealing with live situations, not separating out the compartmentalised subjects of traditional business education courses. Educational practice has followed this by providing courses that are integrated. Case studies provide an ideal means of delivering courses of this nature.

Cases can take several different forms. These can be:

1 situational – the information in the case is analysed and the problem is to be solved.
2 case history – a description of past events requiring analysis.
3 sequential – a case that unfolds in stages. As one situation is analysed another is issued.
4 live – information about an actual organisation (often doctored) is given for analysis.

They should all give a description of a situation and be capable of analysis. Cases should lead to different routes being taken to generate many alternatives with several solutions being given as possible answers. This contrasts with an exercise, where there is one ideal solution. This aspect of case studies often confuses students as they expect that there is one correct answer to a situation or problem and they search for this in vain. At the presentation stage students should be told that there is no one correct answer and it is for them to come to a justifiable conclusion.

Guidelines for teachers

Case studies can be used for both learning and assessment/examination purposes. Overall, case studies should improve the student's ability to make good decisions and improve their judgemental abilities. The process of running a case often involves the student having to defend their statements and opinions and such challenges are useful, if sometimes harrowing experiences, from which the student should learn much. This will involve character building and provide a sound base when they meet similar situations in their work.

As a teaching method they should develop the student's skills in the following areas:

1 analytical – the ability to classify, organise and evaluate information.
2 application – of knowledge, concepts, principles, techniques, etc.
3 creativity – generating alternative solutions and new ways of looking at situations.
4 communication – presentational, discussion, leading, supporting, arguing, reporting, synthesising, etc.
5 social – group working, listening, supporting, guiding, controlling, conflict resolution, etc.
6 self-analysis – building up belief systems, having them challenged, defending beliefs.
7 problem solving – the ability to define and solve problems.

The role of the tutor changes in running case studies. In traditional, didactic teaching, the tutor is dominant and active and the student subordinate and passive. With case studies the roles are reversed to a certain extent where the tutor is there as a facilitator, counsellor, helper, prodder, supervisor but has lost overall control by letting the students get on with the exercise. Cases always need justifying in terms of how they meet course objectives. They should never be used as an extra or put in 'for a change'. Cases should make sense and fit into the scheme or a learning programme.

Prior to a case being run:

1 The tutor should be familiar with the case and the exercises and have a clear idea of the kind of outcomes they are looking for.
2 The purpose of the case should then be made explicit to the students. To issue a case and say 'get on with it' is poor educational practice and potentially disastrous.

3   After reading through the case the students should be given the opportunity to clarify any points on the case, without the tutor giving too many hints on the exercise itself.

4   At the end of the session the tutor should bring the case to an end by reviewing the outcome of the case (perhaps the students having made a presentation on this) and explicitly extracting the main learning points of the exercise. While there may be no set answer the students should have a clear idea about the learning outcomes.

The cases in this book have a number of exercises attached to them. It is not anticipated that all of them will be used together but tutors will choose from the exercises the ones that are appropriate. Clearly the exercises can be amended to suit particular needs. Having given a range of possible exercises this will provide a useful basis for learning activities or stimulate the tutor to generate their own exercises. Some cases have two stages to the exercises to enable them to be developed a stage further. Tutors may wish to go straight to the second stage or carry out only the first stage. The tutor must select according to purposes he/she has set for the exercise overall.

Selecting a case study

1   It should be relevant to what is being taught. It should be an integral part of the course, not a mere adjunct.
2   The case should contribute to the aims of the course. It should have some identifiable aim or cover some learning objectives of the course or unit.
3   The timing of running the case should be planned. It should come at an appropriate point in the course where it can be used to maximum benefit.
4   The length of the case needs consideration. The time taken should not be disproportionate to the learning achieved.
5   The chosen case should be appropriate for the students in terms of their level of ability and the skills to be utilised. It should seek to use their knowledge and experience and be rigorous but not beyond the capabilities of the students.
6   The learning outcomes of the case should be specified so that the tutor can identify to the students what they should get out of it. The students may be required to make an individual presentation or a group presentation or the outcome may be a piece of written work.

Guidelines for students

1   Organise the information. A case contains a large amount of information and this needs to be digested initially. A case should be skip-read first, to absorb the main themes then re-read in detail to collect all the finer details. A further re-read may be necessary when the tasks or exercises have been given. Clarification may be necessary at this stage to ensure that any ambiguities are cleared up. It may be useful to put the headings in order, or to restructure the information to give some coherence to the case. A summary of the main points can be helpful, but care must be taken not to extract a summary and then never refer to the text again. Finally at this stage, differentiate between what is substantiated fact and mere opinion. Opinions can be challenged later on, especially in the light of facts.

2 Specify the problem areas. The problems that appear in the case, and there are often several, should be written down. Some may need clarifying, others may be very difficult to find. Once written down the problems should be classified. This can be in rank order of importance. Problems of fundamental importance should appear at the top and the least significant at the bottom. Doubtless many of the problems will be linked and this can be shown. There are various techniques available to show linkages, e.g. a tree diagram which goes from the 'root' to the 'branches'. At this stage thought should be given to sorting out symptoms and causes. Several minor problems may all stem from one cause. Classifying problems into these two categories, symptomatic and causal, is very hepful.

3 Generate alternative solutions. At this stage the emphasis is on looking for all the possible solutions to each of the problems specified in Stage 2. Nothing should be excluded at this stage, even though it sounds unworkable as a practical solution. There are techniques for this from the formal questionning techniques associated with method study (applying the question why? to the who, where, when, what and how of the situation) to brainstorming and lateral thinking sessions. Creativity is a key skill that should be exercised. It may also be useful to employ any techniques that have been learnt, e.g. analytical or quantitative techniques. Several solutions may be linked and one solution may solve several problems. The solutions can be classified from the general through to the specific.

4 Predict and evaluate outcomes. This is the 'what if' stage. The question to apply to the alternatives generated is 'what if this alternative were implemented?' The basis for selecting a particular alternative solution is whether it provides the best solution to the problem. Some alternatives may create other problems, some just don't solve the problem, others are not practicable etc. Where data is used, each alternative can be evaluated, e.g. costing out various alternatives, say, in a pay claim. The listing of outcomes will then form the basis for selecting the solutions required to solve the problems. There should also be an estimate of the likelihood of that particular outcome occurring. Not all outcomes will occur with the same degree of certainty.

5 Choose the final solution. The pros and cons of each preferred alternative are listed. The solutions that overall are adjudged the best or most beneficial are the solutions that will be implemented. This stage involves comparing the alternatives with each other to allow the final choice to be made.

6 Communicate your choice to the people concerned. After the choice has

been made the solutions have to be communicated to those who have to put them into operation and to those who are affected. This stage is crucial in practice. Often managers may well have made a good decision but they fail to communicate it properly. Frequently in industrial relations, disputes arise not because of the decision but the manner in which it is communicated (or not). Several of the cases in this book illustrate this. The processes of consultation, meetings, information bulletins, etc. are necessary for the successful completion of an exercise. Several exercises require the student to communicate the results orally or in writing. Such skills are essential to successful management.

Summary
1 Organise the information.
2 Specify the problem areas.
3 Generate alternative solutions.
4 Predict and evaluate outcomes.
5 Choose the final solution.
6 Communicate your choice to the people concerned.

Brief summary of cases

Case 1 The annual wage negotiations

This case examines the background and build up to an annual pay negotiations. The setting is a unionised clothing manufacturing concern. The
case details the positions of the two sides, the intelligence gathered and the
pre-bargaining manoeuvres. Sufficient detail is given for students to carry
out some realistic negotiations. The exercises are based on the role play of
the negotiations and also require an analytical report on the situation. A
second stage is given where the outcome of the negotiations is stated and
the participants have to take the negotiations into the next stage.

Topics: consultations, local agreements, disclosure of information, sanctions, wage negotiations.

Case 2 Growing pains

This case examines the growth of an organisation from very small (two
employees) beginnings into a medium-sized firm. The case is based on an
insurance brokerage as it expands both its services and its branch network.
There are the inevitable changes and difficulties and the case emphasises
the need for good industrial relations practices and for the development of
proper procedures and channels of communication. The case also examines
the issue of introducing trade unions and their recognition.

Topics: change, sex discrimination, expansion, negotiations, organisation policy, terms and conditions, unionisation, union membership, union
recognition.

Case 3 Defective procedures are harmful

This case demonstrates the need for good working procedures that are
adhered to by everyone. In particular, the need for disciplinary procedures
and for them to be consistently applied, is emphasised. The firm is a trans-

port contractor and the case gives details of four cases of discipline and the problems that arise. The background detail is of importance and the exercises require the student to solve the immediate problems and to recommend changes that will avoid similar problems in the future.

Topics: Code of Practice on Disciplinary Procedures, criminal record, disciplinary action, disciplinary agreement, dismissal, employment law, health and safety, organisation, procedural agreement.

Case 4 Sorry, you're redundant

This case is based on a firm whose labour force is contracting. Changes in the market and in technology have forced many firms, including this one, to shed labour. This puts the firm's industrial relations under real pressure, tests the skill of managers and how procedures should be used in such circumstances. The case illustrates 'how not to do it' and requires the student to suggest how it should be done. This tests both communication and human relations skills.

Topics: change, consultations, disclosure of information, employment law, negotiations, procedures, redundancy.

Case 5 Going to arbitration

While industrial relations within a firm may be good, there is always room for improvement. The case is based on a retail chain store which has developed some very good industrial relations practices. A need is identified for a formal link to arbitration in the current procedural agreements. A process of consultation has been initiated and the case requires students to examine the proposals given and to recommend a final form of agreement. A range of issues is raised, including the various forms of arbitration, by different groups within the organisation.

Topics: agreements, arbitration, consultations, pendulum arbitration.

Case 6 Technology agreement

This exercise requires the student to examine a set of proposals for a technology agreement from either the union or the management point of view and, after a period of preparation, to negotiate an agreement. The case aims to teach the skills of negotiation and to enable the student to thoroughly investigate the details of the changes instanced by technological change and how firms might solve these problems.

Topics: change, health and safety, negotiations, procedural agreement, technology.

Case 7 Union membership agreement

This exercise requires the student to examine a set of proposals for a union membership agreement from either the union or the management point of view and, after a period of preparation, to negotiate an agreement. As with Case 6, this case aims to teach the skills of negotiation. In addition it enables the student to thoroughly investigate the issues surrounding the closed shop and how some of the contentious points can be resolved, usually through compromise.

Topics: ballots, Code of Practice on Closed Shop Agreements, closed shop, employment law, job grading, legal aspects, negotiations, unfair dismissal, union membership.

Case 8 Disciplinary procedure

This exercise requires the student to examine a set of proposals for a disciplinary procedure from either the union or the management point of view and, after a period of preparation to negotiate an agreement. As with Case 6, this case aims to teach the skills of negotiation. In addition it enables the student to thoroughly investigate the legal and procedural issues raised by disciplinary action and how the issues can be resolved and made into a workable agreement. As discipline is so often a current issue in organisations, this case focuses on the practical and procedural aspects. If the procedure is defective this will lead to problems.

Topics: Code of Practice on Disciplinary Procedures, discipline, disciplinary action, disciplinary procedure, dismissal, employment law, negotiations, procedural agreement, sanctions, warnings.

Case 9 Catering for the workers

This case is based on a hotel and catering organisation and looks at the problems associated with a low paid, high labour turnover industry. Also included are employee rights for minimum wages through Wages Council Orders. The firm is non-unionised and personnel policies are rather rudimentary. The case requires the examination of the problem when managers are confronted with a claim for the firm to pay the minimum wages required by law. There are then a series of other repercussions and further problems to be solved.

Topics: employment law; negotiations, organisation, pay claim, personnel policy, union membership, union recognition, Wages Councils.

Case 10 Breaking the mould

This comprehensive case examines in detail a typical, traditional engineering firm. The organisation is very formal and the firm has been in existence for 80 years. A number of factors forces the firm to change its ways but this meets with resistance. Finally the firm is taken over and the new owners demand rapid change very quickly. Needless to say this leads to confrontation and the case requires an examination of the situation, proposals to alleviate the problem and how to progress in the future.

Topics: change, consultations, custom and practice, demarcation, multiunion firms, organisation, poaching, shop steward, single union agreement, spheres of influence, working practices.

Case 11 The mushrooming problem

This extensive case is based on a medium-sized chemical company where the management is seeking to change some inefficient but entrenched working practices. The case elaborates on the organisational structure and the manager's approach to changing the situation. There is an inevitable confrontation and strike. The case requires suggestions on how to effect a return to work and how to improve the situation in the future by handling the situation in a different manner. The case includes a dismissal and a tribunal claim.

Topics: change, conciliation, consultations, disciplinary action, dismissal, dispute, organisation, shop steward, strike, working practices.

Case 12 Custom and practice

This short case is based on the age old problem of the 'extended' tea break. A manager tries to break the 'bad', old practices. He attempts to bring the length of the tea break into line with agreements and falls foul to claims of custom and practice. The way in which the situation is handled leads to an instant walk out. Students are required to suggest solutions to the dispute and to say how they would have handled the situation.

Topics: agreements, change, custom and practice, dispute, interpretation, strike.

Case 13 The high-risk driver

This case examines a novel problem in which it becomes impossible to continue employing a goods vehicle driver, even though the firm may wish to! The driver's appalling driving record makes him into a non-insurable risk. In the end this leads to his dismissal, with the firm asking for a signed disclaimer against a claim for dismissal. The firm is made to do something it should have done a lot sooner. The exercises take the matter through the next stages involving letters, meetings and a tribunal hearing.

Topics: Code of Practice on Disciplinary Practice, conciliation, disciplinary action, dismissal, safety.

Case 14   Temper! Temper!

This case deals with the problems associated with a manageress of an administrative unit who has difficulties in dealing with her staff. The company are aware of the problem. They refuse to allow her to resign but in the end employee pressure forces her to. She then claims constructive dismissal. The exercises then take the matter through the next stages by gathering information for each side and then making a judgement on the claim.

Topics: constructive dismissal, job performance, managerial action, organisation.

Case 15   Strangers at work

This case involves a mixture of a claim for a closed shop, alleged racial harassment and employees fighting. The union has had a successful recruitment drive and is making a claim for a closed shop. This move is not supported by a minority racial group who then feel that they are being victimised and their jobs are being threatened. This ill-feeling spills over into a minor act of violence and the whole issue surfaces. The exercises require the student to solve the disciplinary problem arising from the fight, the issue of recognising the closed shop and the improvement of race relations within the firm.

Topics: Code of Practice on Racial Discrimination, closed shop, disciplinary action, racial discrimination, union membership, union membership agreement.

Case 16   The unsuitable shop steward

One of the most delicate industrial relations subjects in a unionised environment is how to treat a shop steward. Clearly there is always potential for accusations of victimisation when action is taken against a shop steward. This case examines the situation where a firm refuses to accept the credentials of a duly elected trade union member as a shop steward. There are grounds for this but it creates a very difficult situation which requires some careful handling if the matter is not to become a dispute difficult to resolve. The exercises commence where the elected member has unsuccessfully tried to act as steward for his group. The student has to suggest how the situation should be handled to minimise disruption but bring about a fair settlement.

Topics: credentials, custom and practice, recognition, shop steward.

Case 17 The shop floor worker

This case deals with sex discrimination and equal opportunities in a medium-sized firm. The case raises many of the common issues arising from the anti-discrimination legislation and the subsequent Code of Practice. Many of the firm's policies are discriminatory, albeit not by design but by effect. The case also considers the situation when equality has been achieved but practical problems remain. The exercises are in two stages. The first requires the student to recommend changes that are necessary to bring the firm into line with good practice and the second stage to deal with a particular incident that has arisen.

Topics: equal pay, Code of Practice on Equal Opportunities, custom and practice, job descriptions, job grading, seniority, sex discrimination, recruitment, selection and promotion's policies.

Case 18 Drunk and disorderly

This short case looks at a situation where two employees are treated differently by their boss. There is a reason for this but one that will not placate the employee who feels she has been unfairly treated. The case raises the fundamental issue of treating everyone in a fair and reasonable manner and about being consistent. The exercise asks the student to analyse the situation and to make recommendations to overcome the present problem and to improve practices within the firm.

Topics: competence, disciplinary action, discrimination, procedures.

Case 19 The skittles player

This short case examines an incident in which an employee has clearly breached works rules regarding time-off but it implicates more than the employee himself. The exercises require the student to decide what disciplinary action will have to be taken against the offenders – a brief but significant test of how to tackle disciplinary action sensibly.

Topics: discipline, disciplinary action, procedures, rules.

Case 20   Redundancy at Toolcraft

This case is based on a small, sub-contract engineering firm that, as a result of competitive pressures, has installed some new equipment that has led to the need to reduce the labour force. Although quite carefully handled, the situation still gets out of hand, and when the selected person is given his notice there is a walk–out. The exercises examine how the situation was handled and require a solution to the current problem and suggestions for future policies in handling redundancies.

Topics: closed shop, consultations, dispute, procedures, redundancy, strike.

Table of topics covered

Topics	Case	Case	Case	Case	Case	Case
Agreements	1	3	4	5	10	12
single union	10					
Arbitration	5	8	12			
pendulum	5					
Change	2	4	6	10	11	12
Closed shop	7	10	15	20		
Code of Practice	3	7	8	13	15	17
Competence	14	18				
Conciliation	11	13				
Consultations	2	4	5	10	11	20
Credentials	16					
Custom and practice	10	12	16	17		
Demarcation	10					
Disciplinary	3	8	11	13	14	15
action	18	19				
Disciplinary agreement	3	8				
Disclosure of information	1	4	6			
Discrimination						
racial	15					
sex	2	17				
Dismissal	3	7	11	13	14	
Dispute	11	12	17	20		
Employment law	3	4	7	8	9	17
Equal opportunities	17					
Health & safety	3	6	13			
Job grading	6	7	17			
Negotiation	1	2	3	4	6	7
	8	12	16	17		
Organisation	2	3	9	10	11	14
Pay claim	1	9				
Poaching	10					
Policy	2	9	17	20		
Procedures	2	3	5	6	8	18
	19	20				
Recognition	2	9	16			
Redundancy	4	6	20			
Rules	8	19				
Sanctions	1					
Single union agreement	10					
Shop steward	10	11	16			
Strikes	11	12	20			
Technology	6	20				
Terms and conditions	1	2				
Union membership	2	7	9	15	16	
Wages Council	9					
Working practices	10	11				

Case 1
The annual wage negotiations

Analysis

One of the fundamental elements in our system of collective bargaining is the annual wage negotiations. They determine a large proportion of the terms and conditions of an individual's contract of employment, so that, depending on the outcome of the negotiations, this alone will meet the aspirations of the employees or not. The organisation is also greatly affected by the outcome of the negotiations. The level of pay award and the conditions of employment will determine the charge the organisation has to make for its product or services.

Pay negotiations are a difficult time within organisations with one or other side trying to maintain the upper hand and score points over the other side. Both sides are trying to signal – often a considerable period of time in advance of the negotiation date – what they are looking for in the deal. Added to this pay negotiations are complex, with the topics under consideration not merely restricted to pay but encompassing hours of work, holidays, holiday pay, sick pay, overtime rates, unsocial hours allowances and many other local items.

This case examines the lead up to the annual pay negotiations of a typical company. It looks at local negotiations at workplace level, which is where most employees feel involved. Practice varies but most organisations have some element of locally negotiated terms.

Background knowledge

Before starting this case you should have some prior knowledge of:

1 the nature of collective bargaining;
2 the basis of pay/wage negotiations;
3 the information used/needed by both sides;
4 the arguments utilised in pay bargaining;
5 the process of and tactics employed in negotiations;
6 the sanctions available to management and trade unions to secure a bargain.

Introduction

The annual pay negotiations were due to take place at the Eastern Clothing Co. The pay settlement date for the conclusion of the negotiations was 1 March. Traditionally talks start well in advance of this date and they have always been concluded prior to this date. The company is unionised, with a membership of around 60 per cent of the workforce. The range of topics within the remit of the negotiations has expanded over the years and now covers virtually all the terms and conditions of employment for the members.

Negotiations are conducted locally between the personnel manager, production executive, works director and three union representatives. The firm is a member of an employers' association though not a particularly active one. The district officials of the union are not involved in the negotiations. Usually exploratory talks are held in January, soon after the Christmas break. These are then followed by more formal talks held over the next month to six weeks. The timetable for the negotiations is agreed at the time.

Pay awards over the last few years have been about average for the industry but have not been excessive compared with other industrial groups. The workforce believe that they are soon due for a bumper increase to make up for the lost ground of recent years. For the production department, average earnings, including bonus, are £125 gross. The standard working week is 39 hours, with 18 days holiday a year (plus statutory holidays) which increases to 20 after 5 years' service. Holidays are paid at base rate. The company have not made anyone redundant in recent times, which is good for the industry. The numbers employed have remained constant for the last few years.

Commercially the company is reasonably successful and has maintained its share of a fiercely competitive market. The company produces mainly for the home market and concentrates on fashion wear. This means that it has to follow the trends in the market place and there have been a number of precarious times when the firm has awaited the outcome of the latest launch of fashion wear. Profits are again average for the industry but productivity has been declining in recent times and the firm is examining ways of increasing efficiency. This will mean the introduction of more sophisticated machinery that gives greater adaptability and more output per employee.

Pre-negotiation manoeuvres

The opening shots of this year's campaign were fired by the employers. They reported that the Christmas sales of their products had been disappointingly low and that there would have to be a period of restraint.

With the firm being in the fashion market such fluctuations in the fortunes of the firm are common. This time the company has said that the underlying trend is towards a downturn in business and the future is looking rather gloomy. The managers have taken great pains to ensure that everyone knows about the situation and they all seem to have a very similar tale to tell. Overtime has been cancelled for all but a few of the very urgent, outstanding orders and employees have been warned that there will be little overtime available in the near future. Any extra output will have to be achieved within normal working hours.

The union response to this was low key. There is a great deal of seasonality to the trade and they are used to such tales of despondency. However, one or two members at a recent branch meeting said they felt that the management seemed especially convinced that things were not so good,

---

THE CLOTHING WORKERS' UNION

Eastern Clothing Branch

28 January 19--

Mr B Lambert
Managing Director
Eastern Clothing Ltd
West Street
Wiltonbridge

Dear Mr Lambert

At our recent branch meeting we discussed the formulation of our pay claim for the next round of pay negotiations. We are finding it increasingly difficult to enter into sensible discussions with the firm about the terms and conditions of employment as we have so little real information about the firm. Our District Official spoke to us and stated that as a union we are entitled to much more information than you give us at the moment. We are legally entitled to this information and it would help us to negotiate more effectively.

In particular we request the following information:

(a) earnings analysis of groups of employees; hours worked; rates of pay; etc.
(b) manpower plans for the year ahead; labour turnover statistics.
(c) investment plans; capital expenditure planned; for what purpose.
(d) financial information - profits, margins, earnings, etc.

Awaiting your reply.

Yours sincerely

W Green

W Green
Senior Steward

thus this might not be a bluff. The same meeting went on to consider proposals from the stewards relating to the information made available to them by the management. The senior shop steward, who chairs the branch meetings, had received a document from the district officer which explained the type of information a trade union could request from management for the purposes of collective bargaining. He felt that in the past the union had been negotiating at a considerable disadvantage because it did not have access to the same information as management. Frequently the union had to take the word of the managers regarding the state of the order book, being unable to verify this as fact. The same went for the level of profit made by the firm. The meeting agreed to send a letter to the Managing Director to request that certain information be made available (see p. 3).

Gathering information

There was no reply to this letter. The union guessed that the request, never having been made before, had caused a stir amongst the managers. The union continued its usual lines of enquiry, through its trade union colleagues at local firms, to ascertain the level of pay settlements locally. It also collected some information on the indicators of the cost of living, such as the Retail Price Index.

The company in the meantime had lost no time in preparing itself for the pay talks. It also contacted local firms and tried to gain some infor-

---

Extract from the February edition of Clothing News, the Managing Director's article entitled 'Tightening our belts'

I always wish to be open with the employees at Eastern Clothing and give them the facts relating to the current situation facing the firm. The present picture is, I say with great sadness, not a very rosy one.

We did not do very well in the run up to Christmas, traditionally one of our better times, and things are not looking too well for the Spring season either. We are facing very stiff competition from home and abroad and the contracts that we are securing are at such a low price that there is very little profit in them at all.

... If we are going to move into a period of prosperity as a firm then I have to say to you that we all need to pull together. This may well mean in the near future all the things we may want may have to be delayed until we see better times ahead.

... Another fact that is affecting all firms is the new, high technology equipment that is now being used by some firms. These machines are very efficient but also very costly. We may have to look at introducing some of these machines at Eastern Clothing if we are going to keep up with the competition.

... Finally, I wish to record my thanks to the employees that have contributed to the success of the firm over the years but have to say that these efforts, and greater, will have to be given if we are to remain in business.

mation on local pay settlements and also collected the official figures on the Retail Price Index.

The company has a staff newsletter which is published every two months. The February edition, as with other editions, contained information on the company's fortunes and plans (see opposite page).

The edition was received very coolly by everyone and created an air of gloom and despondency. Casual enquiries for further information made to the managers elicited a polite but unspecific response.

Pay claim formulated

A joint shop stewards meeting discussed the issue and concluded that the article might be an attempt to plant information prior to the annual pay

---

THE CLOTHING WORKERS' UNION

Eastern Clothing Branch

10 February 19--

Mr B Lambert
Managing Director
Eastern Clothing Ltd
West Street
Wiltonbridge

Dear Mr Lambert

We have all read your article in the latest edition of the firm's magazine. As a union, we are very concerned about some of the issues raised and the implications for employees of this firm. You seem to be indicating that the firm is going through a difficult time and that there will have to be changes made. As a union we feel we ought to be more involved in any discussions right at the start if these involve our members.

In particular you mention lack of orders, increased competition, lower profits, improving efficiency and a hint (that frankly was insulting to our members) of slack working and people not pulling their weight. As a union we wish to see the firm succeed and we have always sought to act in that manner. As a union we are seeking clarification on these issues and, in conjunction with my earlier letter requesting information, ask you to supply us with information on these matters.

Looking for an early reply.

Yours sincerely

W Green

W Green
Senior Steward

---

talks trying to create an atmosphere conducive to a low settlement. The meeting also resolved to write to the Managing Director to ask him to clarify the situation (see p. 5).

The same meeting formulated the basis of the pay claim for the formal talks, due to start next week. This was based on:

1 an all round increase on base rates of 10%;
2 a reduction in the normal working week to 38 hours and a commitment to subsequent reductions over the next two years to 36 hours;
3 a consolidation of bonuses into base rates for the purposes of calculating holiday pay and sick pay; and
4 20 days annual holiday for everyone.

There were also some smaller points made regarding the operation of the bonus scheme and the allocation of overtime.

Towards negotiations

As a result of the article in the house magazine and in the build up to the negotiations, the shop stewards have been particularly active. They have raised various matters as official complaints, under the complaints procedure, where normally they would have let supervision deal with the matter. This has been confirmed by the supervisors who have noticed that prior to a complaint being made, employees, who could have raised the matter with their supervisor, have chosen to ignore them and to go to the shop steward direct. This has led to aggravation, as the complaints procedure requires that the originator takes the matter to their supervisor initially and, that if nothing happens, they can then take it to management through their shop steward. The kind of topics raised have included many concerns over safety in the departments followed by the issuing of veiled threats about what might happen if nothing was done.

The reaction of management has been one of stalling and playing for time. They accept that this is all part of the campaign and privately wish that the MD had never written the offending article. They have been careful to listen politely to the complaints and to take note of what has been said. The difficulty is that the procedure requires a reply within the time limits set down or the matter is taken to the next stage. If the wage negotiations were protracted this would create a huge backlog of complaints to be processed. All this can become very time consuming and frustrating. The problem, which all the managers recognise, is that one of the complaints might become the subject of a dispute which would only jeopardise the wage negotiations.

Unofficial soundings taken on the shop floor, by the supervisors, have revealed that many of the employees are genuinely concerned for their jobs. Their prime objective in the forthcoming negotiations seems to be securing improvements in the bonus scheme. The bonus scheme has always been seen as a means of improving the level of individual earnings and much of the work indeed provides the means of doing so. This information has been passed to senior management.

Another piece of useful information has come to the attention of the senior steward. The telex operator was overheard talking to her friend about a series of telex messages that she had been dealing with recently. Her friend was the cousin of a shop steward and she casually passed on the information. The steward then made a few more discrete enquiries and encouraged his cousin to speak with the operator again. It transpired that the firm was in the advanced stages of negotiating a very large order with a multinational shopping chain. By dint of fortune this information was confirmed in separate reports coming from the sales office.

Talks begin

On Monday of the first week in February the negotiating committee met for the first time. The meeting started with the union making an opening statement which contained the claims mentioned above. They also stated that the current figures available for the Retail Price Index showed that inflation was currently running at 8%. They also declared that their intelligence from local firms showed that wage settlements were running at 8% and moreover this was in firms that had a higher base rate figure to start with. Some firms had a base wage of £135 a week for operatives (on a 38 hour week) and they also enjoyed 20 days holiday a year (on average earnings). The senior steward noted the great concern that the firm had found it fit to start a campaign based on fear of job loss and had not replied to the letter requesting information. He also said that even though they were not privy to the state of the order book, they had it on good authority that there was a lucrative order in the offing. The union side said that they were unable to negotiate sensibly in the absence of the facts and figures. Such facts as were divulged at the negotiations were selective and likely only to be those that supported the management's case. They needed the full range of facts on which to make a balanced decision.

The management reply to the opening statement by the union was to reaffirm the position outlined in the house magazine. There was a definite downturn in orders and this looked likely to be the case for the foreseeable future. Where the union had got its reliable (quote) information from, the management could not see. Much as they would like this to be the case, it was not. In reply to the statements about the rate of inflation, the personnel manager said that the figure quoted was the rate for the previous year but the official forecast for the coming year was a much lower rate of inflation, more like 5%. She also said that their information on local pay settlements was at variance with the union's information. While one firm had settled at 8%, it was because it had just recovered from a severe decline in business and was allowing for an element of catching up. The clothing trade had never been able to pay high rates as the business was so competitive and open to foreign imports. The best the firm could do would be to hold on to what it had and have a year in which everyone consolidated their positions.

The final statement to the meeting by the senior steward was that if the management were not able to make a very definite offer which could be considered to be an improvement then he would have to report to the union meeting on the next day that management were not negotiating seriously. It would be very difficult for him to contain the reactions of the members and he could not be responsible for the problems that might ensue. It was agreed that another meeting would be held on Friday morning. The production executive said that, as a final statement from the management side for that meeting, he would like to end on a positive note by saying that there was a need to improve productivity. This meant there was room for increasing output related bonuses if the union was prepared to negotiate improved working practices. However, this did not mean that there was any room for manoeuvre on base rates or anything that added to overall costs with no related increase in output.

After the talks

The subsequent union meeting was indeed the stormy affair that the senior steward had predicted. A number of the employees wanted the negotiating committee to tackle the problem of base rates and holiday pay as a priority. Some of the more vociferous members asked for a commitment from the meeting that, in the event of no movement on base rates, the members should institute some form of industrial action. This was never put as a motion and was not taken as anything other than a few members letting off steam. Nevertheless they had some support. The meeting broke up with the stewards instructed to pursue the claim on base rates as a priority.

Shortly after the union meeting the supervisors heard stories about the real possibility of industrial action. This information was passed on to the senior managers. A further complication for management was that the large order that the union had got wind of had now been finalised. The exact terms of the deal were only known to two senior people in the sales department and the Managing Director. The order would provide work for the production unit for some considerable time. It was not due to start for six weeks but then would be steady work.

Exercises

Stage 1

1 The personnel manager is concerned that the negotiations are not going at all well. She contacts you, as a fellow personnel officer and member of the IPM. The request is that you act as an unofficial industrial relations consultant to the firm. Prepare a report, as the consultant, on how you think the firm should conduct the negotiations from now on. In addition, make recommendations on how the firm should conduct its industrial relations which would improve wage negotiations.

2 The senior steward contacts his district official to report on the proceedings and subsequent union meeting. The official decides to call on the firm the next day. As senior steward, make notes on the important features of the situation, as you see it, and list the options open to the union for the next stage of the negotiations.

3 As the district official after being briefed by the senior steward, make detailed notes on how the union ought to proceed in the next stage of the negotiations. Utilise the information raised in Exercise 2.

4 The Managing Director contacts the local employers' association to ask for their advice. He is concerned that the pay negotiations are entering a difficult phase. Draft the letter to the Association and draft a reply from them to the Director. If you are in a group 'send' the letter to another member of the group for a reply.

5 In groups, enact the next meeting of the negotiating committee. Prior to this, meet in separate union/management groups to decide your strategy. Select the roles each will play, based on a formal negotiation committee, i.e. chairperson, secretary, spokespersons etc. If possible video the proceedings. Prepare an agreed statement at the end of the official proceedings, including the next stage of the negotiations, if agreement is not reached.

6 As a member of a small group of trade union members, examine the possible forms of industrial action that the union could take. List these and evaluate them in terms of effectiveness, acceptability to the members and costs to both sides.

Stage 2

The next meeting of the negotiations committee makes some progress but there is a final failure to agree. There has been agreement on the following:
1 across the board 7 per cent pay increase;
2 consolidation of average bonus earnings but not average overtime, for holiday pay only;
3 19 days annual leave, rising to 22 days after 5 years of service.

The sticking point has been the claim for a shorter working week. The firm is adamant that it cannot afford to reduce the working week any more. It points out that the additional cost is too great and that the employees would only make it up in overtime anyway. The average working week within the firm is about 44 hours. When the basic working week came down from 40 to 39, the average working week did not change. The union counter claim that all the local firms in the area are now committed to a reduction in the working week with most on 38 in the current year and agreement to reduce to 36 or 37 hours in stages over the next few years.

1   At a meeting of the management side of the negotiating committee, formulate your strategy for the next stage of the negotiations. Decide how far you are prepared to go in sticking to your point or whether there is any room for bargaining.

2   The branch meeting held following the breakdown of negotiations has given its backing to the union negotiators to secure a reduction in the working week. The meeting did not decide on any specific sanctions that might be taken but gave a remit to the negotiators to take what action they felt was right. Meet as the union representatives and formulate your strategy for the next stage in the negotiations. Decide how far you are prepared to go to secure your stated aim, what you may be prepared to bargain on and what sanctions you might envisage threatening or using.

3   Convene a meeting of the negotiating committee to thrash out the remaining issues. Take it that both sides have said that this is the very last meeting on the issue and agreement must be reached or it is deadlock. Again run the meeting formally with people nominated to specific roles. Prepare an agreed statement at the end of the meeting.

Case 2

Growing pains

Analysis

As organisations expand there are always growing pains involved. One way in which this manifests itself is the need for structure and formality in staff relations. With a small number of people the managers can deal with individuals on a one-to-one basis and there is a great deal of flexibility. The structure of the organisation is undefined and adapts to suit the moment. There is little need to define roles or to have rules to define conduct within the organisation. Wages can be decided as between employer and employee.

As an organisation employs more people the need for a more formal structure becomes apparent. Rules are needed to deal with all employees in a fair and consistent manner. Difficulties arise particularly when a hierarchy emerges and each manager is required to treat their employees in similar manner. To remain without a structure for long when the organisation is growing, can lead to problems, which if they are not solved will lead to difficulties. The following case illustrates the sort of problems that can ensue in what is otherwise a flourishing firm.

Background knowledge

In this case you are required to examine an organisation during a period of growth and to analyse the problems that emerge.

Before starting this case you should have some prior knowledge of:

1 organisational structures;
2 the role and function of management, particularly policy making;
3 communication structures, consultations and negotiations;
4 human relations and motivation;
5 trade union recognition, recruitment and membership.

Starting up

Fifteen years ago Peter Robinson and his long-time friend Jim Lyons, decided to leave their employment with a national insurance firm and set up their own business. Having spent ten years of their working lives in the industry they felt the time was ripe to go out alone. They live in a relatively prosperous area in Cambridgeshire and were convinced that given a lot of hard work, they could establish a prosperous business. They set up an office in a small, rural town to sell car, household and life insurances along with personal investment schemes. Their respective experiences in insurance were complementary as were their characters. At first they employed part-time secretarial help as needs arose.

Through hard work and determination the business prospered, albeit with the occasional hitch. After three years they set up a second branch in a town nearby. They were then employing a number of secretarial staff and recruited young people to train up with the business. The pattern of work established in the branches was a reflection of Peter and Jim. They expected their staff to work hard and to high standards, impressing on staff that the continued existence of the firm, and its future growth, depended on building up a satisfied clientèle. If they were working beyond what is considered to be normal working hours they would expect staff to do so until the work was finished. Any staff not doing so were soon given a clear message that they were not the type of employee wanted in the firm. Peter in particular could be very direct and not a few staff had felt the sharp end of his tongue. In return those staff that did a good job were rewarded with pay rises and promotion.

Personnel

The idea that staff should be flexible was positively encouraged. If help was needed in a particular area then staff were expected to move in to help. A typist would act as receptionist, a receptionist would do some filing, a clerk would answer the phone. This was taken as normal practice and staff in general liked this as it gave them the opportunity to move around the office and carry out a range of tasks. Holidays had to be taken to suit the business and Saturday morning working was normal.

Over the next few years a number of other branches were opened and Peter and Jim took in junior partners to act as branch managers. As the network extended Peter and Jim spent more time away from the branches, working on the bigger deals with local firms for their insurance needs and building up a specialist investment service. This meant that more of the day-to-day decisions of running the business were delegated to the branch managers. Gradually they were allowed to recruit staff and run the branches as they saw fit. Certain decisions had to be referred to Peter or Jim where certain expenditure was involved or where there were difficult technical problems. The branch managers were very much in the mould of Peter and Jim, demanding high standards and dedication. This led to tensions within the branches as the staff, particularly the newer ones who did not know Peter or Jim very well, looked on the job as a regular one with normal, fixed hours of work. The labour turnover was higher than could be expected even allowing for the relatively young age structure of the staff. Grumbles were frequent but there was no formal channel for these to be vented.

Organisation

The structure of the firm was rather chaotic with there being no formal staff grading or wages structure. After ten years in business the firm employed 45 people but Peter and Jim found a large proportion of their time was spent on developing the network of branches and diversifying the services of the firm. This meant that little attention was paid to internal affairs, but providing this did not interfere with their plans, then they saw little need to do so. Neither partner thought there was anything wrong with the business as it continued to expand and produce a handsome level of profits. The younger, ambitious staff, who were being trained in the insurance business, tended to stay with the firm as they saw the prospects with a smaller, expanding agency as a better prospect than working for the big insurance companies. Any conversation with them would not have revealed any problems, as they did not have the same perceptions as the clerical and secretarial staff. It appeared to all the staff that Peter and Jim were doing very well out of the business. They both had expensive cars, had purchased large houses and were able to holiday abroad.

The practice had always been for staff to be transferred between the various branches. This was part of the flexible approach the firm encouraged and was useful to staff, as it gave them a wider experience of other branches and to the firm, as it gave them a pool of staff to draw on. Transfers occurred during holiday periods or when there was a long-term absence. The system worked tolerably well but was not liked by those with local commitments after working hours. Travel on public transport in the area was difficult; the firm did not contribute to any increased travelling costs incurred. Transfers also gave staff the opportunity of exchanging information on the conditions of work at other branches and it soon became apparent that a wage policy did not exist. Also practice seemed to vary from branch to branch. Anyone transferred for any length of time soon had a grievance if they suffered any inconvenience as a result of the transfer.

Incidents

One young man from one of the branches was asked to go to another branch some distance away the next week. He said that he would find that difficult as he did not have transport and he already had a long journey into work. The manager insisted on him going and the young man, being rather timid, reluctantly agreed to try to get there. On the Monday following he did not arrive until 10.30 (instead of 9.00) and was reprimanded by the manager. The young man was not given any opportunity to explain the situation to the manager who was new to the area. It happened that Peter was at that branch that day and being under pressure told the man that if he ever behaved in that way again he would be sacked.

Another incident concerned a young woman, a secretary at a branch, who was pregnant. Unfortunately the pregnancy was a difficult one and she had to have days off frequently or had to go to see the doctor. She carried on with the firm but was advised by her doctor to leave employment and have a protracted period of rest. The baby was due in about 15 weeks time. On informing her manager she requested that her job be left open for her, as there was the possibility, especially in this case, that there might be complications. The manager replied that the firm did not have a policy of keeping jobs open because they needed to be certain of where they stood with staffing. After thinking the matter through the woman resigned under protest. Later she lodged a claim for constructive dismissal which was turned down because she had not been with the firm for two years.

The new trainee

About two years ago Phillip was appointed a trainee at one of the branches. He had worked for a large insurance company and was felt to be an asset to the firm because of the training he had received with his previous firm. Unknown to the manager who appointed him, Phillip was a strong trade unionist and had been an organiser for the Insurance Staff's Union at his previous place of work. While not a militant, he stood up for people's rights and would air grievances on behalf of others. It was soon apparent that he would stand up to the manager and Peter where he felt there was a genuine grievance. His work was fine but clearly he had gained a reputation of being a bit of a stirrer. Secretly he went around other members of staff soliciting their support for the information of a union within the firm. This was helped by the fact that his job required him to travel around the branches. Gradually a number joined the union but all this was unknown to any of the managers.

About 20 staff had already become members of the union. Phillip then took the step of making a formal claim for recognition of the union by the firm (see p. 15).

The reply received by Phillip from Peter is shown on p. 16.

10 October 19--

Mr P Robinson
East Anglian Insurance Co
North Street
Fenbridge

Dear Mr Robinson

I am writing to you to make a formal request for union recognition. In
particular, it is for you to recognise the Insurance Staff's union as
representing the staff of East Anglian Insurance. Currently about 20 of
your staff are members of this union and it would make sense if these
employees had their membership officially recognised to enable the
union to perform its function properly.

The reason for the request is that it is now clear that the firm needs a
union that can represent the views of the staff to management. Many of
the aspects of industrial relations would improve if there were a union
that could speak on behalf of its members. It would also provide a means
of taking up matters with management and entering into some collective
agreements on things like pay and conditions of work. The object of the
exercise is not to create a division in the firm but to make for smoother
running within the firm.

I would ask you to consider this request. I would welcome the opportunity
to discuss this matter with you.

Looking forward to your reply.

Yours sincerely

P Marks

P Marks

Exercises

Stage 1

1 You have been appointed the personnel consultant by Peter and Jim. Prepare
the report referred to. The terms of reference are to investigate the situation in
the firm with particular reference to the need or otherwise for a trade union and
to make recommendations on the means of improving industrial relations within
the firm. Within the report note the methods you would use to carry out such an
exercise.

2 You (or a colleague) are Phillip. State what you would do in the circumstances. Given that you will co-operate with the investigation, what evidence and
suggestions would you give to the consultant? Submit this in the form of a
memorandum.

THE EAST ANGLIAN INSURANCE COMPANY

Fenbridge

19 October 19--

Mr P Marks
C/o North Street Branch
Fenbridge

Dear Mr Marks

Thank you for your letter of 10th October.

We have considered your request for union recognition at East Anglian
Insurance. Our initial response to this request is a firm <u>no</u>. We
consider there is no place for a union within East Anglian Insurance.
The management of this company is well able to conduct its industrial
relations and employee relations without the need for a trade union.
It is our experience that trade unions do not help and in many ways
hinder. Our managers can be consulted at branch level and they can
consult with us on matters they are not able to deal with.

We are somewhat disturbed that you (or others) have been recruiting staff
into a trade union. This has been done behind our backs and we feel
insulted that we have not been informed about this until now. We would
remind you that we are the owners and managers of this organisation and
before any changes are made authorisation should be obtained <u>before</u>
action is taken. We are requesting that you inform us of those that have
joined the union.

However, as you have highlighted an area where we recognise that potentially
improvements could be made, we will employ a personnel consultant, part-time,
to investigate the firm's policies and to make recommendations.

This investigation would be open-ended and the consultant would have a free
hand in what he/she recommended.

Finally, a decision on the request to form a union in the firm would be
left until the report has been received.

Yours sincerely

P Robinson

P Robinson
Director

---

3   The consultant asks to meet Peter and Jim to ask them questions about the
development of the firm and their personnel policies. Prior to the meeting Peter
and Jim meet to discuss their approach. Write notes that they would make in
preparation for meeting the consultant. You are free to make whatever assumptions you wish on what stance they may make with regard to the issue of trade
union recognition.

4   As part of the exercise the consultant wishes to ascertain the feelings and
attitudes of the staff on a number of issues. He/she has made an appointment

to come to your branch tomorrow. You have been asked to be the speaker for your branch, having been with the firm for some time and being respected by your colleagues. Write some brief notes on the situation from the employee's point of view and what you would recommend should be done.

5 Acting as Jim Lyons, you have been told of the two incidents (referred to on p. 14). Having elicited the facts of the two cases you analyse the situations with a view to making some conclusions regarding the running of the firm. Draw up such a short report.

Stage 2

The consultant's report has been published. It does not state whether a union should be recognised or not but suggests that the firm should institute systems that would allow this type of decision to be made. The report recommends that the firm should institute some kind of consultative system where the employees, at the branches, can become more involved in the business. The consultant mentions Briefing Groups as a possible system, providing the managers use them as a means of two-way communication to feed information back up the line.

```
12 January 19--


Mr P Robinson
East Anglian Insurance Co
North Street
Fenbridge


Dear Mr Robinson

Thank you for your letter of 19th October.  I have also seen the
consultant's report.  It seems largely inconclusive and does not
address itself to the central question originally raised, ie, trade
union recognition at East Anglian Insurance.

I have talked to many of my colleagues and have been asked to re-submit
a request for union recognition of the Insurance Staffs' Union at East
Anglian Insurance.  Currently 45 per cent of full-time staff and 30 per
cent of part-time staff are now members of the union.

I do not accept your criticism of going behind your backs in recruiting
members.  This is a decision for the individuals concerned and employees
have the right to join a union if they so wish.  Clearly many of the
employees have decided they wish to join and they have not been coerced
into this.  It seems to reflect the existence of a problem which you
cannot sweep away.

I am requesting a meeting with you as a matter of urgency to discuss the
recognition of the union at East Anglian Insurance.

Yours sincerely

P Marks

P Marks
```

THE EAST ANGLIAN INSURANCE COMPANY

Fenbridge

16 January 19--

Mr P Marks
C/o North Street Branch
Fenbridge

Dear Mr Marks

Thank you for your letter of 12th January.

Clearly this is not a matter that is going to be resolved through
correspondence. A meeting has been set up for a week on Wednesday
at 10.00 am in my office to discuss industrial relations within
the firm.

This should not be taken as an indication of our intention to allow
trade union recognition at East Anglian Insurance.

Look forward to seeing you at our meeting.

Yours sincerely

PRobinson

P Robinson
Director

Peter and Jim are relieved that the report does not directly recommend the introduction of a trade union and they see the way forward as instituting a consultative structure merely as a sop to the kinds of criticism levelled at them.

Some staff, especially the more vociferous ones, see the report as something of a 'whitewash' which comes to no specific conclusions. They are determined to press ahead for radical changes. They argue that the firm has been criticised and the only way forward is to introduce a trade union in each branch. Phillip is persuaded to make a formal request to Peter and Jim to form a branch of the Insurance Staff's Union at East Anglian Insurance (see p. 17). The reply received by Phillip from Peter is shown above.

1 Role play the meeting between Peter, Jim and other senior partners (keep the numbers down to a total of, say, five) and Phillip, an Insurance Staff's Union official and other employee representatives (again keeping the total to five). The agenda for the meeting should be drawn up by the 'management' side prior to the meeting and 'sent' to the 'employee' side. Put a reasonable time limit on the meeting, allowing sufficient time for the participants to reach a conclusion. At the end of the meeting prepare agreed notes based on the meeting and state the conclusions arrived at.

2 The 'management' group should convene separately and consider the outcome of the meeting. Prepare a plan based on what needs to be done to put into effect the conclusions arrived at in the joint meeting. Pass this to the 'employee' group when you have this ready.

3 The 'employee' group should convene separately and consider the outcome of the meeting. Discuss the next stage in the plan to accomplish your objectives as a group of employees. Consider any communication received from the 'management' group.

4 Finally, reconvene the joint meeting to arrive at a final action plan based on the two groups' considerations of the previous meeting and any subsequent communication. At the end of a time-constrained discussion prepare agreed notes on the conclusion of the meeting (even if it is a final failure to agree).

5 As a branch manager, having read the consultant's report, write an appraisal of his suggestions. Include a further section on how these, or similar suggestions of your own, should be implemented at East Anglian Insurance to improve industrial/employee relations. Work out the practical details of your recommendations.

Case 3

Defective procedures are harmful

Analysis

One of the fundamental aspects of a good industrial relations system is the existence of workable agreements. The process of collective bargaining leads to agreements and it is these which provide the framework within which the cogs of the industrial relations machinery work. The need for agreements is manifold and includes the need to treat everyone with equality and fairness; agreements also provide the procedures that will be used in particular circumstances.

However, the mere existence of agreements does not necessarily mean that all will be well. The agreements themselves will need to be constructed so as to achieve their purpose. Poorly worded or defective agreements can be worse than having no agreements at all. This case examines a situation in which a disciplinary agreement exists but because it is a poor agreement it leads to a number of problems.

Background knowledge

In this case you are required to examine a number of practical incidents, usually relating to discipline, where things would have gone much better if the agreement that existed had been workable and had been used.

Before starting this case you should have some prior knowledge of:

1 managerial authority and responsibility;
2 the construction and working of procedures;
3 problem solving;
4 handling disciplinary action and dismissal.

Another Monday morning

It was an ordinary Monday morning when Alf Ramsbottom arrived at his lorry depot in Felixstow. He was feeling pleased with life as he perused his fleet of new Volvo lorries and the brand new BMW he had indulged in last month. He reflected that life had not always been like this. His father, who had set up the business, had not known such good times but would have been proud to have seen his son succeed in this way. The haulage firm was established in 1932 as a local contractor to deliver goods and farm produce in the area around Ipswich. It had, like all such businesses, had its ups and downs, and tended to follow the fortunes of the economy. The one factor that had caused FleetHaul to enter the big-time league of road hauliers was the expansion of the docks at Felixstow. Alf had many connections locally and had timed his moves to perfection. Just when it was obvious that the future in road transport lay in containerised transport, Alf invested in lorries to take on this business. Through a lot of hard work and much support from his workforce, the firm had grown. They picked up a few, large contracts from the shipping firms and demonstrated their ability to operate throughout the country. The firm had not really looked back since the mid-sixties and all the workforce had enjoyed the fruits of prosperity.

Problems, problems

This feeling of self-contentment did not last long though. Before Alf could enter his office on the Monday morning for a meeting with his managers, he was approached by the yard foreman. Bob was a long serving and loyal employee of the firm but was lately finding the going hard and Alf suspected that Bob was not performing as well as he had in the past. As they met, Alf knew there was a problem; Bob both looked and felt angry. He opened up the conversation, not with his usual pleasantry, but dived straight in. 'It's now two weeks since I asked you to look into this question of men arriving late on week-ends. I can't be here all the time to make sure they behave themselves. You know that if we are not at the docks on time, we are in lumber. And I tell you, we had a right load of trouble on Saturday. Same set of drivers, turning up when they think fit, not when we want them in. You said you'd have them on the carpet straight away and tell them that there's no week-end driving for those that can't get here on time'.

This rather threw Alf for a moment, as he could not remember what Bob was talking about. Then he recalled that Bob had said something to him last week about the lateness of the week-end drivers but did not recall having promised to do anything about it. Anyway, he felt that it was for the supervisors and managers of the firm to deal with those kind of day-to-day problems; he was there to secure orders and deal with the customers. 'OK, Bob I can see that this is bothering you, I haven't the time to look into these matters myself and you know that as foreman you can deal with such incidents as a matter of discipline, after all we have got a procedure for that kind of thing. We have to use it or the union will have our guts for garters'. Bob replied: 'But you know that the procedure is not worth the paper its written on. When did we last issue a warning and make it stick. We either get soft and let them off or we get the union coming down like a ton of bricks and you, and the others in there, back down. No use us doing anything if you lot won't back us'. Alf was not a born diplomat and had survived in a notoriously rough trade, but he was usually courteous to his senior staff and expected them to be the same. In particular he found Bob's attack out of character. 'I will raise the issue at our weekly meeting which I am late for now, and we will decide what needs to be done. I'll let you know soon' and Alf strode off to the office.

His reaction was one of mild irritation. These small, fiddly problems always seem to get in the way and detract from the important business. He hoped that perhaps the meeting of his managers would help put this behind him. It was all right casting him in the role of big boss but he thought he had sorted the organisation out sufficiently well to see that problems of that nature were dealt with without reference to him. The firm was unionised and they had seen to it that there was an agreement on things like discipline (*see* Appendix on p. 26). Why couldn't people just get on with things!

Safety standards

His mood was to slip into one of greater irritability at the manager's meeting when the same topic was brought up. The garage manager, Chris, said that it was time to air a few internal grievances from the managers. He said that he, and a number of the other managers and supervisors, had all noted that the standard of discipline in the firm was slipping and this was having a detrimental effect on the firm as a whole. He related a situation regarding health and safety rules in the garage that was becoming almost impossible to deal with. Certain jobs in the workshop were dangerous and there were procedures which should be followed and protective equipment which should be worn. Recently there had been a lowering of standards and in spite of constant vigilance by the supervisors, it seemed the situation was still declining.

Chris said 'Last week I had a welder in my office and gave him a stern private warning that if he was found welding without wearing the correct goggles he would be disciplined and that could lead to him being taken off welding work, which is, as you know, well paid, and I'd put him on a lower grade job. The only reply I got from him was that the procedure did not allow for safety to be a matter of discipline. Blow me down, if later that day the steward didn't come in and tell me that if I tried disciplining his members on the grounds of health and safety, he'd take out an official complaint against me!'

The problem recognised

The meeting then spent a little time discussing the situation generally, with the consensus being that things were indeed getting worse but some merely commenting that it was all a sign of the times.

A final piece of 'any other business' came from the Office Manager, Sally. She said that she was of the opinion that the firm was in difficulties all round with discipline. Sally had been with the firm only one year and couldn't comment on the decline but came upon a number of incidents that she had found hard to deal with because there seemed to be no uniform system of handling discipline. Her item related to the fact that she had had to withdraw a disciplinary warning against a member of staff, for persistent lateness, because Sally had not invited her friend in with her when Sally had issued the warning. Sally said she knew of no such requirement, especially as the offices were not unionised, and felt that her authority had been undermined early on in her job at FleetHaul. The procedure made no reference to being accompanied by a friend or shop steward at a disciplinary interview.

The sacked criminal

Later that week the Transport Manager had an official appointment with the shop steward of the drivers' union. The firm was a virtual closed shop on the driving side of the business. The steward was a driver himself and had been with the firm for several years. He always drove a hard bargain but was also fair and would always seek a solution to a problem. Previous meetings, which were held quite regularly, had been fractious and sometimes heated, but the men respected each other.

The steward opened the meeting by saying that he was most alarmed about the difficulties that seemed to be arising in recent times. One case he wished to raise as an official complaint was related to the dismissal of a driver the previous week. The case was a very sad one and concerned a driver who had been found handling stolen goods; he had then been committed to a Crown Court for trial. There was no evidence that the goods had been stolen from FleetHaul. The driver's name was revealed in a court report and the Transport Manager had interviewed the driver the following day. The driver obviously had little to say about the offence but the Manager explained that the firm could not employ anyone who had acted suspiciously as customers would be reluctant to have anyone deliver their goods who was a suspected criminal. At the end of the rather tense meeting the Manager had dismissed the driver and given him four weeks' pay in lieu of notice. The case had aroused strong feelings amongst the drivers and had the yard not been so busy and the drivers occupied on long-distance deliveries, the incident could have led to a serious dispute.

Fortunately the temperature had dropped but the steward was still talking in terms of reinstatement for the man, pending the outcome of his trial. There were veiled threats that if the firm was not prepared to reconsider then there may well be a dispute arising and possibly union action. The Transport Manager had heard similar talk before but had the difficult job of deciding how much was bluff and how much was serious. The steward went on to state, in detail, that at the recent union branch meeting there was a great deal of resentment that the driver had been sacked. The steward ascertained that the driver had been told as soon as he walked in to the disciplinary interview that the case was open and shut and little could be said except to go through the motions of saying why he was being sacked. The Manager did not dissent from this account. Asked why the driver still had not received written confirmation of the dismissal nor a statement of the reasons for the dismissal, the Manager said that there seemed little point now but he would get round to it if the steward insisted. The meeting resolved nothing on the question of the sacking and the steward decided to see if anything happened as a result of the meeting and, if nothing did, to pursue it further and vigorously.

Persistently late

The steward decided to rub salt into the vexed question of discipline. He then raised the case of Tom. This was not as serious as the one of the sacked driver but was another example of management's ineptitude and blundering. Tom was a yard assistant who had previously worked for the firm as a driver but for the last six years had been in the yard on general duties. He had one weakness in life; his love of beer. This had caused a number of problems to him over the years, not least a difficulty in getting up the morning after a session on the beer. There had been no known incident where his drinking had affected his driving, because he just never turned up the next day. Tom had been given a verbal warning for lateness 15 months ago during one of the firm's clamp-downs on timekeeping and absenteeism. The yard supervisor, who kept records of lateness and absenteeism, had called Tom into his office last week and issued Tom a final written warning (see opposite).

The steward observed that if the lateness and absenteeism had been persistent over the last 15 months, it seemed a little late in the day to issue

```
                              FLEETHAUL

                  LONG DISTANCE HAULAGE CONTRACTORS

                             FELIXSTOWE


  M E M O R A N D U M


  TO:        T Barnes
             cc A Ramsbottom, Shop Steward

  FROM:      Transport Manager              DATE:   25 January 19--


  SUBJECT:  Final Written Warning



  This is to record that on 22 January 19--, after an interview with you, I
  issued a final written warning to you.  Over the past year you have been
  late on 54 occasions and a total of 650 minutes late and you have been
  absent on 18 separate days over this period.  This is totally unacceptable
  and if there is no improvement in the next six months further disciplinary
  action will be taken.

                    T. Reynolds
  Signed:
  T Reynolds
```

another warning. Also, a 15-month gap between warnings meant that the first warning had now been wiped off the record and Tom would be starting with a clean sheet. Anyway, the firm had tolerated Tom for 24 years and he was part of the culture of FleetHaul. While not everyone could act like Tom it seemed harsh to expect a man of 63 to give up suddenly the habits of a lifetime.

The Transport Manager reported all this to Alf when they next met. They both expressed concern that the business was begining to get bogged down with a number of niggling incidents and that one might lead to a major problem one day.

Exercises

1   Analyse the incidents in the case and prepare a report for Alf Ramsbottom stating what your analysis of the problems is and prepare a list of specific recommendations for action by him and his managers.

2   The steward reports the outcome of the meeting with the Fleet Manager to his District Official. As the District Official, reply to the steward recommending what the steward ought to look for in the new procedure. Also give advice on what the steward should do about the outstanding problems.

3 The managers have decided that the problem of discipline at FleetHaul now calls for some serious attention and remedies. The first step has been a call for a full Managers' meeting, which Alf has agreed to. Prepare notes for when you attend this meeting, as a manager at FleetHaul. What issues will you raise and what is your analysis of the situation?

4 A small committee of three managers has been formed to review the outstanding cases of disciplinary action. Examine the four cases recorded and make recommendations on what action should be taken in those cases or similar ones occurring in the future.

5 At a second stage the firm have decided to retain a personnel consultant to advise the firm on the disciplinary procedures and how discipline is handled in the firm. As part of your remit, examine the current procedure in use at FleetHaul and state in what respects it is defective and what problems it is likely to give rise to. Prepare a consultant's report with recommendations.

6 Draw up a disciplinary procedure for use at FleetHaul. Apply the procedure to the incidents that arise in the case and state what the outcome would have been if a good procedure had been used properly.

7 As a training advisor to FleetHaul, draw up a training programme that you think the managers and supervisors should undertake to implement the new procedure. Concentrate on the topics that should be covered rather than the methods of delivery. Using the incidents recorded in the case as illustrative material, construct a 'compare and contrast' exercise for the members of the training programme.

Appendix

FleetHaul Ltd
Disciplinary Procedure

This agreement will be used for all cases of disciplinary action.

STAGE 1 – A manager or immediate supervisor shall issue a verbal warning, specifying the behaviour that is unacceptable.

STAGE 2 – If a verbal warning has been issued, then if there is a further breach of discipline the manager or supervisor shall issue a final written warning.

STAGE 3 – If there is a further breach of discipline or the employee has committed a serious breach of discipline the manager can dismiss that person.

Warnings shall be taken off the record if no further warnings are issued within 12 months of the issue of the previous warning.

Case 4

Sorry, you're redundant

Analysis

One of the problems that many organisations have had to face in recent times is that of how to reduce the number of employees in a firm. The occupational structure in the country has changed much in the post-war period, with the traditional industries declining – such as cotton, wool, railways, mining and shipbuilding – because of changes in technology and competition. Other industries have been radically affected by technological change where highly productive machinery and equipment has displaced slower, inefficient labour intensive methods. Finally, economic factors have prevailed which have necessitated firms having to employ fewer people because of the downturn in demand.

Whatever the cause, the situation is not an easy one for any organisation to face. It causes morale to slump and individuals have to face a very difficult situation. How organisations approach the question of redundancy and how they process them, is an area that needs a great deal of attention and skill. This case examines a redundancy situation in detail and raises a number of questions relating to the subject.

Background knowledge

In this case you are required to analyse a redundancy situation and to suggest how the case should have been handled. Times of redundancy are always difficult periods in any firm and they need handling in a very sensitive way. Before starting this case you should have some prior knowledge of:

1   the grounds on which employees can be made redundant;
2   the consultation procedures that should be utilised;
3   how redundancies should be declared;
4   what help employees should be given;
5   the law relating to redundancies;
6   the role of a trade union in this situation.

The firm

It was a normal Friday afternoon at Sheetmet Co. The personnel in the Production Department were cleaning up the area after the day's work and sorting out paperwork. Everyone was looking forward to the weekend, especially as there was a social club fishing trip the next day. The operators, supervisors and managers got on well with each other and many of them saw each other outside work. The pace was slowing down, as it tended to on a Friday afternoon, as there was no point in starting any work before Monday and the machines were always in need of a good clean.

Sheetmet was a firm of specialist sheet metal workers who made prototype work for a variety of industries and also carried out small batch work. They prided themselves on their skill. If it could be made of sheet metal, Sheetmet could do it. The firm employed 80 people but even at this size was friendly, with everyone, from directors downwards, on first name terms. The firm was clearly not in an expanding market with the competition coming from non-metallic substitute materials, which were easier to fabricate than metal and altogether more attractive to· designers. Nevertheless, it had maintained a healthy order book for most of the past ten years. However, recently those leaving, mainly through retirement, had not been replaced and it had become noticeable that there was an aging workforce with few young people entering the trade to provide succession.

SHEETMET CO

MEMORANDUM

TO: All Staff

FROM: Peter Thompson, Managing Director   DATE: 6 November 19--

The Board have examined the future position of the company and regretfully announce that, due to the disappointing performance in the current financial year and the poor state of the order book, there is a need to reduce the workforce of the firm.

We have considered how best to implement this decision and have concluded that in the production department the last ten people joining the workforce are to be made redundant. These are .....

Arrangements will be made on Monday morning for these people to be paid in lieu of notice.

Peter Thompson

PJT/skl

The declaration

Without anyone being particularly aware a notice appeared on the notice board. The board was full of posters, notices, minutes and informal notices but the new, clean sheet was conspicuous (see p. 28).

(see p. 28)

There was a stunned silence as the word went round the department and everyone gathered round the notice board. People found it difficult to know what to say, especially to those affected by the redundancy notice. The supervisor was called over and he denied any prior knowledge of the notice. He could see the reaction of the group and went off to see his boss. He ascertained that the production manager and all the other managers were at a meeting, but no one knew where. Not one for giving up, he went to the Directors' offices, only to find the doors firmly locked.

The selected few

Of the ten listed on the notice board, seven were under the age of 30 and had been with the firm less than two years. They had all received training within the firm and were considered to be skilled operators. It was commented that within the department there were six men who were within three years of retirement. They had casually commented that, had they been asked, they would cheerfully have volunteered for redundancy.

The same evasiveness persisted on Monday. Meetings seemed to be held everywhere and no one could be contacted. The ten men listed on the notice reported to the wages office where they were given their money. The situation did not improve when it was learnt that only two people were being made redundant from the offices, one of them being a part-timer. Eventually a deputation from the Production Department met the Managing Director. He went over the matter again in more detail and while fully sympathetic, said that there was nothing to be done. He was clearly agitated by the severe criticism of his handling of the situation. It was not the first time that he had had difficulty in dealing with problems that might lead to confrontation. This incident had occurred four years ago and had remained firmly in the memories of all.

The current position

The company continued to maintain a reasonable level of activity and the workforce was down to 60, other losses occurring through natural wastage. However, the recession was biting hard. Technical changes had meant less sheet metal work was needed and the future was looking gloomy. At the end of the financial year the firm was in the red and the projection for the next year was poor. Unless remedial action was taken, the firm, the accountant advised, was in danger. As 60 per cent of the direct costs were labour costs, it seemed inevitable that a reduction in human resources would be necessary. On this occasion the shop floor had become aware of the impending decision. Requests were made for information but the replies were evasive and vague. One lunchtime the employees organised an informal meeting in the canteen. At the meeting it was decided that the management should be approached officially.

Exercises

1   As the unofficial representative for the group you were very much involved in the redundancy incident four years ago. You reflect on this experience to formulate some ideas for the immediate situation. Write a short, analytical report on the original redundancy incident and draw up a 'lessons to be learnt' set of recommendations.

2   Management have agreed to meet a delegation of employee representatives in two days' time. Meet as a group of employees and draw up an agenda for that meeting with management. Specify the information that you will be seeking from management.

3   You will be involved in the meeting with the employees in two days' time as a manager. The Managing Director has tasked you with finding out the legal requirements relating to redundancy and to send a memo to him on this, in layman's language.

4   You have also sought the advice of a personnel specialist on how a potential redundancy situation should be handled. Write a set of notes on the main points of what would constitute good working practice in this situation. You are particularly concerned about minimising the impact of reductions in human resources. Explore the range of possibilities available to the firm and list them.

5   Write a procedure for dealing with a redundancy situation, including the means of communication, notice to be given, consultations and the level of compensation to be offered.

6   Use this scenario as the basis for a joint negotiation exercise. Each side, employer and employees, should prepare their case first, then negotiate an agreement to cover:
    (a) consultation procedures;
    (b) the methods to be employed to minimise the effects of redundancy;
    (c) the basis of selecting people for redundancy;
    (d) the mechanism for processing redundancies.

7   Use the agreement from Exercise 6 to deal with the situation that currently exists with regard to the necessity of reducing human resources to maintain the firm's viability.

Case 5

Going to arbitration

Analysis

While the majority of matters arising within firms are dealt with and disposed of either unofficially or by using agreed procedures, there always are a few issues that are ultimately difficult to resolve. Even with the best procedures some very difficult problems might remain unresolved. When procedures have been exhausted and there is nowhere else to go, the dispute can continue and cause immeasureable harm to the organisation. Often it is at this stage that the dispute spills over into industrial action. To provide a way out of this impasse many procedures allow for arbitration or some other means of third party intervention to resolve the dispute. This case examines this process in detail by looking at the issues that are raised when referring cases to arbitration. While it is unlikely that all the points that are raised in the case would occur in any one firm, it provides a realistic scenario in which to examine these issues.

Background knowledge

In this case you will be examining the detail of referring disputes, grievances and unresolved questions raised in negotiations to arbitration. It will raise some issues of principle and also the practical points on how such references would work in practice and be incorporated into existing agreements. You will be required to look at the topic from several viewpoints.

Before starting this case you should have some prior knowledge of:

1 collective agreements; their structure and content;
2 the methods availabe for third party intervention to resolve disputes and outstanding questions;
3 the detail and possible variations in arbitration clauses;
4 pendulum arbitration; its use and possible benefits;
5 the similarities and differences of approach to arbitration by various groups, within an organisation.

Going to arbitration — Introduction

Brandwells is an old established grocery firm that has survived the massive changes that have taken place in the retail trade and has become a successful firm. The company own 40 branches in the South-East,

---

SHOP WORKERS' UNION

South-East District Office

4th February 19--

Mr P Brandwell
Brandwell Grocery Co
High Street
ROCHESTER

Dear Sir

Please find below our suggestions for a scheme of arbitration that could be included in the agreements we have with you.

1   Arbitration can be triggered off at any time when it is apparent that no further progress can be made, ie, a failure to agree has been registered.

2   Any settlement is entirely voluntary. The arbitrator's recommendations can be accepted, amended or rejected.

3   There can be an application for arbitration by either side where it appears to that side that no progress is being made.

4   The choice of arbitrator is to be agreed jointly.

5   The statements of case are to be submitted to the arbitrator first and then exchanged when he has received both statements.

6   There is to be a maximum time limit of three weeks between a reference to arbitration and the receipt of the arbitrator's report.

7   No legal representation is allowed by either side and only one advisor per side. Those entitled to attend are those who represented the sides at the last stage prior to the reference to arbitration.

8   The arbitrator's report can be published to all interested parties.

9   Both sides are bound to co-operate with the arbitrator, to meet him, make submissions and to be questioned.

Yours faithfully

M Porter
Shop Steward

---

employing 200 full-time staff and 400 part-time staff. The firm has a very professional personnel function that has encouraged trade union membership within its branches and has consultation procedures to involve staff as much as possible in the firm. The recognition of trade unions has led to a number of collective agreements on various topics. There is a dispute and grievance procedure as well as a negotiating procedure. These have all worked well and industrial relations are considered to be very healthy.

The need has now arisen for these agreements to be improved. Recently there have been one or two incidents that have not been resolved by the procedures and have only been finally resolved with a great deal of hard work. The suggestion has been made that the agreements need a final stage adding that allows for third party intervention. Both management and unions have agreed on the principle of the need to incorporate such a change and in particular that some form of arbitration should be used. The next stage is to work out the exact means of achieving this. The current state of play is that both sides have gone away to think out their respective positions on the proposal. Opposite and below are the suggestions that have been formulated, but none of the groups that are being consulted have put their proposals up for discussion yet.

BRANDWELLS

MEMORANDUM

TO: Personnel Department

FROM: Store supervisors and Store Managers DATE: 5 February 19--

SUBJECT: Arbitration Clauses

As a result of the working party set up to draw up a recommended set of clauses on arbitration, we submit the following:

1 A reference to arbitration should be the last stage in the procedure, when all other stages are exhausted.

2 Any settlement to be agreed by both sides, based on the recommendations made by the arbitrator.

3 Any application for arbitration should be a joint one unless a failure to agree has been registered for three weeks.

4 The statements of claim by management should be approved by the local managers before being sent to the arbitrator.

5 There should be a time limit of three weeks between the reference to arbitration and the receipt of the arbitration report.

6 A representative of the local branch management should be allowed to be heard or make representations for disputes arising from their branch.

7 Hearings should be at the source of the dispute.

Shop Workers' Union

1 Arbitration can be triggered off at any time when it is apparent that no further progress can be made, i.e. a failure to agree has been registered.

2 Any settlement is entirely voluntary. The arbitrator's recommendations can be accepted, amended or rejected.

3 There can be an application for arbitration by either side where it appears to that side that no progress is being made.

4 The choice of arbitrator is to be agreed jointly.

5 The statements of case are to be submitted to the arbitrator first and then exchanged when he has received both statements.

6 There is to be a maximum time limit of three weeks between a reference to arbitration and the receipt of the arbitrator's report.

7 No legal representation is allowed by either side and only one advisor per side. Those entitled to attend are those who represented the sides at the last stage prior to the reference to arbitration.

8 The arbitrators report can be published to all interested parties.

9 Both sides are bound to co-operate with the arbitrator, to meet him, make submissions and to be questioned.

Supervisors and Store Managers

1 A reference to arbitration should be the last stage in the procedure, when all other stages are exhausted.

2 Any settlement is to be agreed by both sides, based on the recommendations made by the arbitrator.

3 Any application for arbitration should be a joint one unless a failure to agree has been registered for three weeks.

4 The statements of claim by management should be approved by the local managers before being sent to the arbitrator.

5 There should be a time limit of three weeks between the reference to arbitration and the receipt of the arbitration report.

6 A representative of the local branch management should be allowed to be heard or make representations for disputes arising from their branch.

7 Hearings should be at the source of the dispute.

Head Office Management/Personnel Department
1 The reference to arbitration should be made only when all the stages of the relevant procedure have been exhausted, and a final failure to agree has been registered.
2 The award of the arbitrator is fully binding on both sides, without amendment.
3 Applications for arbitration shall be made jointly.
4 The arbitrator shall be chosen from a list supplied by the Institute of Arbitrators and that person be approached to act.
5 Statements of case to be exchanged before submission to the arbitrator.
6 There is always a need for flexibility and no time limits will be imposed unless jointly agreed between both sides.
7 Either side is entitled to be represented by whom they wish at the hearing.
8 The final award will not be published to anyone except those directly concerned.
9 Attached to the clause on reference to arbitration is a clause that no industrial action will be taken while the matter is still under consideration. Any such action will cease while the matter is under reference.
10 The hearing shall be held at Head Office.

Personnel Advisor's Suggestion
An internal report from a personnel specialist has recommended that agreement be sought on the following points:
1 when arbitration should be used and at what stage;
2 whether the settlement is binding or not; and if the recommendations can be the subject of further negotiation;
3 who can make application for arbitration;
4 how the arbitrator will be chosen;
5 if statements of claim are to be exchanged and when;
6 any time limits;
7 the right of representation;
8 the publication of the arbitrator's report and its circulation.

In addition the advisor had also suggested that the sides might wish to consider the use of pendulum arbitration. (This is where there is a normal reference to arbitration but the statements of claim are the basis of the recommendation by the arbitrator. The function of the arbitrator is to choose between the two statements but without amendment. Hence the award will be to accept the statement of either one or other side.)

Individual exercise

1   The three sets of proposals have been sent to you at the Institute of Arbitrators. As an industrial relations advisor, critically appraise the proposals and send a report to all three parties on the form and content that the arbitration clause/agreement should take. Provide the reasoning behind your recommendations. Provide an alternative report on the use of pendulum arbitration.

Group Exercises

1   In three separate groups examine the three sets of proposals. Amend the proposals, as the group sees fit, to provide an acceptable set of proposals for that section in the company.

2   After the period of preparation in 1, form a negotiating committee and attempt to reach agreement on the arbitration clauses that could be used in this situation. As you reach agreement on a clause, make a written record of it. Ensure there is agreement on the written clause.

3   Consider, in detail, the proposal for pendulum arbitration. Draw up a separate arbitration agreement based on pendulum arbitration. Again this can be a negotiation exercise, as in 2, with each side preparing their case beforehand.

4   Use the arbitration agreement you have drawn up to resolve the disputes in Cases 11, 12 or 20. Use the facts of the case:
   (a) to draw up agreed terms of reference;
   (b) for each side to make a statement of claim;
   (c) to make any representations allowed under the agreement.
   Finally acting as arbitrator, issue findings on the case.

Case 6

Technology agreement

Analysis

With the rapid changes that are taking place in most organisations there is a need for a framework within which change can take place. One of the effects of technological change is that job content and methods are altered, often radically. There is always the fear that old skills will be displaced and with this the people that possess them. In order to ensure a smooth transition during a period of change an agreement will help resolve the problems by providing a framework within which they can be solved. This case introduces a procedural agreement whereby the decision to implement technological change is made subject to negotiation and joint agreement.

Background knowledge

In this case you will be negotiating an agreement that can be used when change is taking place within an organisation due to an application of technology.

Before starting this case you should have some prior knowledge of:

1 preparing for negotiations and taking part in them;
2 the effects and implications of technological change within an organisation, including job security, job design, organisation, health and safety and training;
3 the management of change;
4 the various views held by different parties on the last two issues;
5 policies and procedures on consultations, disclosure of information and decision making.

Introduction

From a set of proposals you will be required to negotiate a technology agreement. It takes the form of a procedural agreement which can be used in the future when any such changes are proposed. It is not expected that the detailed implications of a particular change are worked out but the agreement will provide a framework within which this can happen.

Management proposals

Aim

The company and union recognise that to ensure the efficiency and prosperity of the industry the most effective systems and equipment should be used with the aim of securing the future of the organisation and its employees.

Procedure

1   The company will use this procedure while new equipment is being introduced to achieve a smooth transition.
2   The company agree to discuss matters relevant to the introduction of new systems and equipment, including working methods, staff levels and training.
3   The company will supply such information as appears necessary to keep employees informed of the systems and equipment to be installed.
4   The company will appraise the unions of changes at the regular meetings that are currently held.

Issues

1   *Job security*   as far as possible the company will ensure that overall no job loss will ensue as a result of technological change.
2   *Redeployment*   as far as possible employees will be offered redeployment elsewhere in the company if their current job is no longer required as a result of technological change.
3   *Redundancy*   the company will offer voluntary redundancy to those who cannot be redeployed or to those who request redundancy.
4   *Job descriptions*   all new jobs will be evaluated and the new terms and conditions will apply to the employees employed in the new positions. Any changes to existing job descriptions will be discussed with the individuals concerned.
5   *Health and safety*   the health and safety aspects can be made the subject of a joint management/safety representative inspection when the equipment

has been installed (as allowed for in the Safety Representatives and Safety Committees Regulations).

6 *Training* such training as is necessary will be provided by the company.

7 *Rewards* the pay of those operating the new systems and equipment will be reviewed in accordance with the current wage review system.

Union proposals

Aim

The company and union recognise that to ensure the efficiency and prosperity of the industry the most effective systems and equipment be used with the aim of providing job opportunities, higher rewards and improved terms and conditions.

Procedure

1 The company will not introduce any new systems or equipment without first having exhausted this procedure.

2 The company will negotiate all relevant matters prior to the introduction of new systems and equipment including workloads, working methods, human resources levels, staffing arrangements, training, career progressions and development, redeployment, changes in the terms and conditions of employment and compensation for any changes resulting.

3 Full information should be given by management to the union, prior to any decision to buy being made, to enable the union to fully appraise the situation. Information to comply with the requirements of section 17 of the Employment Protection Act 1975 and the Code of Practice on the Disclosure of Information.

4 A joint union/management committee is to be set up to deal with the implications of all specific changes in systems and equipment to fully evaluate such changes in detail.

Issues

1 *Job security* there will be no overall loss of jobs as a result of technological change.

2 *Redeployment* any employee whose job is no longer required as a result of technological change shall be offered redeployment in the company with no loss of status and shall be given retraining where necessary.

3 *Redundancy* there must be a minimum of redundancies. Any that occur must be entirely voluntary with payments in excess of the statutory minimum.

4 *Job descriptions* all new jobs must be jointly evaluated between union and management (*see* Clause 4 of the procedure). Any changes to existing jobs to be re-evaluated with no loss of status to the individual performing that job.

5 *Health and safety* all aspects of health and safety to be fully discussed at the safety committee prior to any changes (as noted in the Safety Representatives Regulations and the Code of Practice).

6 *Training* a training programme will be agreed between union and management. All those on training will suffer no loss of earnings during training or retraining.

7 *Rewards* the benefits arising from the use of new systems and equipment will be shared between the company and employees. There should be a planned movement towards a shorter working week, longer holidays and a lower retirement age.

Exercises

1 Initially the union side and management side should meet separately to study their briefs. The proposals given can be added to, deleted or amended. At the preparation stage the arguments in favour of and against the proposals should be thought out.

2 After a suitable period of preparation the two sides should meet to discuss the proposals with a view to reaching an agreement. Preferably treat these negotiations more as a discussion on common ground rather than it being a conflict situation. As you progress agree on the wording of each clause, which should be recorded. In conclusion draft a final agreement based on the clauses recorded.

3 Use your final agreement as a basis for solving Case 20, Redundancy at Toolcraft.

Case 7

Union Membership Agreement

Analysis

During the 1970s there was an increase in the number of closed shops in a number of industries. The traditional 'heavy' industries, such as ship building, mining, steel making and the railways, have had closed shops for a number of years. However, all these industries suffered a decline in numbers employed within the industry, but the proportion of the working population affected by closed shops increased. The increase in closed shops was notable in the food and drink industry, in local authorities, the utilities and other parts of the public sector.

Alongside this change came the introduction of employment legislation that provided a legal framework for the operation of the closed shop and also introduced the concept of unfair dismissal. The latter generated a rather thorny problem in that those who worked in a closed shop but who refused to join a union might, at the insistence of the union, have to be sacked. The employer might then be sued, in a tribunal, for unfair dismissal. The law has variously granted the right not to join a union for certain categories of employee. The grounds for this have included those with religious conviction and those who object on the grounds of conscience. These changes led to a growth in the use of negotiated closed shop agreements, which were given the less emotive title of union membership agreements. Having such agreements has distinct advantages for both sides and provides an open framework within which to operate.

In the 1980s the law was changed to restrict the operation of the closed shop. These laws made it compulsory for any closed shop that was to enjoy any status at law, to be agreed, in a ballot, by the employees affected. Any closed shop that does not have the support of 80 per cent of those entitled to vote is not recognised at law and anyone sacked in that situation, for non-union membership, could sue the employer and the union.

Due to the economic decline and the tighter employment laws, the number of union membership agreements has declined in recent times. However, where closed shops still exist there is still the need for a negotiated agreement for its operation. The following case study is designed to investigate the various factors that need close examination and to negotiate a settlement from a given set of proposals. It raises a number of important and fundamental questions and rarely can the exercise be run without generating plenty of heat!

Background knowledge

This case combines the important aspect of collective bargaining, of negotiations, and the very contentious issue of trade union membership and the closed shop. Discussing the issues that arise coolly and sensibly with people whose views are possibly very different from your own and to reach an agreement on these issues, tests the negotiating powers of the participants to the limit. The case is set in context so that students can use this as a framework within which the negotiations can take place.

Before starting this case you should have some prior knowledge of:

1 preparing for negotiations;
2 negotiating an agreement through from presenting a case to final, written agreement, including the skills of negotiation;
3 the meaning and practice of closed shops and the problems arising from them. Also the various viewpoints on the closed shop and the arguments for and against it;
4 the relationship between the closed shop and dismissing a person for non-membership of a union. This should include the law relating to a recognised closed shop (for the purposes of dismissal claims) and the official Code of Practice on the closed shop;
5 How trade unions deal with applications for membership, their rules on expulsion and the resolution of problems arising.

Introduction

The company is a food manufacturing firm that makes a range of cooked and frozen pies for the fastfood trade. It employs 120 people, with 80 being employed in the production departments. About 60 of the operators are in the Food Workers' Union but there are 10 staunch members of the General Workers' Union. There is a grading structure within the departments and noticeably only members of the Food Workers' Union have been promoted to the top grade. Industrial relations are good but this is not to indicate that the peace is kept easily. Negotiations are hard and long with each side usually taking quite a hard line. Nevertheless the sides respect each other and the Food Workers' Union convenor is respected by both his members and the management.

The thorn in the flesh for the union is that they are desperately trying to achieve 100 per cent membership. In many ways a closed shop operates now but without official recognition from management. The convenor is involved in seeing applicants for jobs and makes clear the need to join the union. In recent times this has always led to the new employee being a union member or becoming one soon after joining the firm. Negotiating agreements are laid down and most matters are dealt with by negotiation.

Management proposals

Preamble

This is an agreement between the Food Workers' Union (the union) and the company for the operation of a closed shop in the production departments, subject to the following clauses:

1   All current non-members may opt to stay out of the union.
2   Grounds for refusal to join the union are:
   (a) religious belief;
   (b) conscientious objection;
   (c) membership of another union.
3   Trainees, apprentices and part-timers are not covered by this agreement.
4   Recruitment and selection remain a management prerogative.
5   New entrants will be given two months to join the union, subject to Clause 2.
6   Workers not complying with this agreement will not be subject to the disciplinary procedure.
7   In any claim in an industrial tribunal, arising from this agreement, the union may be joined in that action (i.e. jointly sued by the applicant).
8   The company will refuse to put any of its employees under pressure to join the union or not.
9   Any unreasonable refusal of entry to, or expulsion from, the union will be referred to the TUC Independent Review Committee.
10 A secret ballot will be held of all the workers covered by the agreement to ensure acceptability of these proposals. An 80% majority of those entitled to vote is required to ratify this agreement. Ballots will be held at 5 yearly intervals to check for continued support.
11 In case of any dispute arising under this agreement, the normal disputes procedure will apply. Additionally, in the event of a final failure to agree, the matter will be referred to external arbitration, which will be binding on both parties. No industrial action will be taken before this procedure is exhausted.

> **Union proposals**
>
> *Preamble*
>
> This is an agreement between the Food Workers' Union (the union) and the company for a closed shop in the production departments to cover all production workers, and that they will be, or become, members of the union subject to the following clauses:
>
> 1 All current non-members to join the union.
>
> 2 All members of any other union to join the union.
>
> 3 Trainees and apprentices must join the union.
>
> 4 Expelled or lapsed members to be disciplined by transfer or dismissal.
>
> 5 The company is to specify union membership requirements on the company's application form.
>
> 6 The shop steward will see all potential employees before they are offered employment.
>
> 7 All sub-contractors working in the department must be trade union members.
>
> 8 The shop steward is entitled to vet all sub-contractor's workers, to ascertain their trade union membership.
>
> 9 Only trade union members are to be employed in the top two grades of employment.
>
> 10 If there are any changes in manpower structure (for example due to technological change) any new personnel will become members of the union.
>
> 11 Trade union machinery will be used to verify the acceptability of these proposals to the work group.

Exercises

1 From the set of proposals negotiate a union membership agreement. Initially the union side and the management side should meet separately to study their briefs. The proposals can be added to, deleted or amended as the participants see fit. It is helpful if the management side do not have an out-right and non-negotiable stance on refusing to have a closed shop! The amount of preparation on working out strategy and tactics pays dividends. Try to have a clear idea on the points that you wish to secure and those that you might 'trade'. Prepare your arguments and try to anticipate the arguments of the other side and prepare your counter-arguments.

2 After a suitable period of preparation the two sides should meet to discuss the proposals with a view to reaching agreement. During the exercise, as you reach agreement on the various clauses, make a written, agreed record of the clause. At the end of the negotiations go through the agreement to ensure it reflects the views of both sides.

3 Apply your final agreement to the situation in Case 15. Strangers at Work.

Case 8

Negotiating a disciplinary procedure

Analysis

One aspect of day-to-day industrial relations that is of great importance is the need to deal with people fairly and consistently in matters of discipline. Many disputes are caused because disciplinary action has been taken against someone that is seen as unfair, discriminatory or victimising. The lack of a procedure leads to arbitrary decision-making and inconsistency. In order to handle discipline in an orderly manner it is good practice to utilise a procedure agreed to and known by everyone. This eliminates possible arguments about the consequences of certain behaviour and the way in which employees are disciplined. On the other hand procedures should not be so rigid that they do not allow some discretion. If the rules are written as 'musts' then they have to be applied no matter what the circumstances are and that can also lead to problems.

Background knowledge

As disciplinary action may lead to dismissal then such action is linked inextricably to the law relating to unfair dismissal. The basic law is quite simple and straightforward. There are complications when it comes to dismissals in a closed shop situation (see Case 7) but this is rather a minor detail and is not important to this case. Additionally, disciplinary action is an everyday matter of industrial relations and all cases need handling with care, not least because a badly handled case might lead to a dispute and legal proceedings.

Before starting this case you should have some prior knowledge of:

1 the process of negotiating an agreement;
2 the preparatory stages prior to negotiations commencing;
3 the use of procedural agreements;
4 the law relating to unfair dismissal;
5 the Code of Practice on Disciplinary Practice and Procedures in Employment.

Union proposals

Preamble

This agreement is to be used in all cases where disciplinary action is to be taken against employees. The object of the agreement is to provide a fair and uniform procedure for dealing with all disciplinary matters.

Procedure

It is agreed that:
1 the issue will be resolved at the lowest possible level;
2 each stage will be completed as soon as possible, compatible with thorough investigation;
3 an employee has the right to be accompanied by a shop steward at all times;
4 at all stages an employee, against whom disciplinary action is being taken, has the right to appeal against that action. During the period of the appeal the action will be suspended. The appeal will be heard by a senior manager not previously involved;
5 a written record of each stage will be made, but only signed by an employee where it is an agreed record;
6 the union reserves the right to take whatever industrial action it considers appropriate at any time;
7 the union reserves the right to suspend this agreement at any time or to amend it by giving one month's notice.

Stages

Stage 1

If the employee has committed a proven minor offence, the employee's immediate superior will issue a verbal warning, but only after the employee has stated his/her case.

Stage 2

If an employee has received a verbal warning within the last month and has committed a further, proven minor offence, the departmental manager will issue a written warning.

Stage 3

If an employee has received a written warning within the last month and has committed a further, proven minor offence, the Director responsible will issue a final warning.

Stage 4

If an employee has committed an act of gross misconduct or has received a final written warning within the last month and has committed a further, proven minor offence, the Chief Executive may, in extreme circumstances, dismiss or suspend the employee.

Management proposals

Preamble

This agreement is to be used in all cases where disciplinary action is to be taken against an employee. The object of the agreement is to provide a fair and uniform procedure for dealing with all disciplinary matters.

Procedure

It is agreed that:
1   the issue is to be resolved at the lowest possible level;
2   the issue is to be resolved within three working days;
3   an employee can be accompanied by a person of their choice, if they so wish;
4   at all stages an employee, against whom disciplinary action is to be taken, can appeal against that action;
5   a written record of each stage will be made by management and a copy sent to the employee. A signature will be required signifying they have received the warning;
6   while the matter is still within procedure no industrial action will be taken by either side;
7   this agreement can only be suspended by management giving six months' notice or amended by giving three months' notice.

Stages

Stage 1

If the incident is a minor offence and the employee has no previous warnings, the employee's immediate superior will interview him/her. The superior will then issue a verbal warning.

Stage 2

If the employee commits a further minor offence and has already received a verbal warning, the employee will be interviewed by their departmental manager. The manager will issue a written warning.

Stage 3

If an employee commits a minor offence and has already received a written warning, the employee will be interviewed by their director. The director will then issue a final warning.

Stage 4

For incidents of gross misconduct or where an employee commits a minor offence and has already had a final written warning issued against them, the employee will be interviewed by the Chief Executive. The employee will then be summarily dismissed.

Agreed notes

Offences

Gross misconduct	*Minor offences*
drunkeness	persistent lateness
fighting	poor attendance
theft	unacceptable quality of work
fraud	incompetence
sexual impropriety	insubordination
clocking in another person	unsafe working practices

For all alleged incidents of gross misconduct an employee will be suspended until the offence has been investigated and Stage 4 of the procedure can be organised.

Exercises

1 In two separate groups examine the proposals as either management or union representatives. The proposals can be amended, added to or deleted as the groups see fit. Prior to negotiation work out your strategy, the arguments you will employ, the points you wish to secure and the ones you are prepared to trade. Look for possible compromises that may be necessary.

2 After a period of preparation the teams should meet for negotiation. Each side should present their case and then discussion should be opened on the points raised. You should assign roles, such as spokesperson and secretary. As progress is made, agree the exact wording of the clauses and make a precise record. As a final stage agree the final wording of the whole agreement.

3 The procedure that you have finally negotiated can be used to resolve the disciplinary or dismissal situations in Cases 3, 13 and 14.

Case 9 _____

Catering for the workers

Analysis

One aspect of the British industrial relations system is that there is *no* standard method of conducting industrial relations. The variety of methods utilised derives from the different situations that various organisations and groups of workers find themselves in and is affected by the history of the industry. In some sectors industrial relations is well developed; in other sectors it is not. Where there is not a well-developed system the State has seen fit to intervene in an attempt to introduce a system of industrial relations. The major reform in this area was brought about by the Whitley Committees (1916–18) which led to the formation of *joint industrial councils* in some industries and, in the sectors not organised at all, to *trade boards*. These latter organisations were formed to set minimum wages and other terms for those working in the sector covered by the Board. These bodies are now known as *wages councils* and still perform the function of setting minimum wage levels. The idea was that after a period these bodies would evolve into negotiating bodies involving representatives from both sides of the industry.

In some sectors the process of collective bargaining has not developed as envisaged and the terms and conditions are still set by the councils. The sectors covered by wages councils include shops, hotel and catering and farming. While *wages council orders* are legally binding there is a problem with enforcement. Inspectors are appointed to check that organisations adhere to the terms laid down in the orders, but clearly they cannot cover all locations. The following case looks at a situation involving the levels of wages in the hotel industry.

Background knowledge

In small firms, in a non-unionised environment, industrial relations is often rudimentary, but there are issues of common concern with workers in unionised, more complex organisations. The basic terms and conditions of employment are fundamental to all employment relationships but how they are determined varies, in particular the extent of the employee's voice and power to determine these.

This case examines a situation in which the employees have very little say in the determination of their pay and conditions and there are no formal means of them being involved. While certain basic statutory rights exist, these may not be known to the employees and not adhered to by the employer.

Before starting this case you should have some prior knowledge of:

1   the role and function of wages councils, including the content of such orders and the means of enforcing the orders;
2   initiating and developing collective bargaining where none exists already;
3   the recognition of trade unions within a firm;
4   resolving matters of dispute without any formal procedures;
5   the law relating to minimum wages and wages councils, in particular the 1986 Wages Act.

Introduction

The Mid-Anglia Hotel Group is a thriving hotel and catering group that has had a remarkable growth rate since its establishment in 1968. The group owns six hotels in East Anglia and performs other catering functions in the region. Its services range from accommodation, bars, restaurants, a club and an outside catering service that is now expanding into contract catering for local organisations. The founder and owner of the group is Chris Glover. His father had been in the same trade and after Chris had graduated from his degree course in hotel catering and management, his father helped him raise the capital for his first hotel. Chris's first hotel venture was a success and this was soon followed by the acquisition of a second hotel. A mixture of being in the right area at the right time, hard work and a good head for business combined to make the group successful.

Workforce

As with the hotel and catering trade in general, the labour force employed by Mid-Anglian is predominantly part-time and casual. About 40 per cent of the workforce is full-time, the balance being permanent part-time or casual labour contracted for special occasions, such as for the outside catering unit and in the banqueting facilities in the hotels. Chris employs some capable managerial staff at the permanent locations and retains them by paying salaries that are high for the catering sector and by giving his managers autonomy in running their establishments. Apart from the managerial staff, the labour turnover is high, as it is for the industry as a whole. This clearly causes problems for the business but it is one which the managers live with.

The staff that the business can recruit is predominantly young and/or female. Without some prospect of stability or promotion, staff will not stay. Also many of the staff move around locally within the trade. Recently the group has taken on a number of YTS trainees and, in conjunction with the managing agents and local colleges, is hoping that this will provide the basis for a stable core of employees. Chris is committed to training his staff to high standards and regrets that much of the good work that the business puts into training its staff is lost through the high labour turnover.

Wages

The personnel function is performed by the individual managers. They recruit and select, discipline and dismiss. The firm looks after its employees reasonably well and the perks of the job are quite good. The staff can retain all tips and, to reduce pilferage, staff are given food handouts. Wages are determined centrally by Chris and his top managers. The trade does not pay high wages but Mid-Anglia are amongst the lowest payers. This frequently causes problems and staff constantly complain that they can get higher pay elsewhere. The firm maintains its workforce because with the high turnover in the trade they replace leavers quickly. The unrest amongst staff has never spilt over into confrontation or dispute but nevertheless there is a problem which everyone recognises. Chris is not prepared to let wage costs increase because he still has plans to expand and looks to the business to generate most of its own capital. He feels that the problem is exaggerated and every firm in the trade pays such low wages and there is general discontent amongst all staff. He believes the firm does look after its staff better than most and this should be taken into consideration. There are no unions recognised in the firm and there are very few union members. There has never been a claim for a union to be recognised.

Irate employees

One day an employee at one of the hotels was thumbing through a Hotel and Catering journal that one of the managers had left around. She started to read an article about wages in the industry. The article said that the latest Wages Council Order had just come into force. Appended to the end of the article was a table of the minimum wage rates that applied to the hotel industry. She was alarmed to see that these rates were higher than Mid-Anglia paid. As she was not too clear on what exactly all this meant, she took the magazine from the hotel to let her husband read it. He read the article and said that it was clear that Mid-Anglia were not paying as much as they should do.

The next day Chris was confronted with an irate deputation of his work-force. They were demanding that the company pays the rates of pay laid down or there would be no meals prepared, drinks served or rooms made ready that day. At the same time three other managers, at other locations, were confronted with the same demands from their employees.

Exercises

Stage 1

1 Advise Chris on what action he should take in the immediate situation.

2 The other managers ring in and relate their story. What advice should Chris give them on what they should do and say?

3 As an advisor to the firm describe, in detail, a practical policy for the firm and what short- and long-term action should be taken by the firm?

4 One of the workers involved contacts the local office of a trade union. The Area Officer arranges a meeting with several of the staff. He recommends that they join the union and then he will claim recognition for the union in Mid-Anglia. They all join and go round recruiting others. The Officer then contacts Chris to arrange a meeting. Write the letter that the officer sends to Chris. As Chris, state what your reaction would be and draft a letter in reply.

5 Given that there is initial resistance to the claim for unionisation in the firm, as Area Officer, what would your tactics be? What arguments would you put to the firm supporting the case for recognition in the firm? What benefits might there be for the firm? Write this up as a letter, restating your claim for recognition.

6 Role play the meeting between Chris and the Area Officer after the letter has arrived.

7 The Union Officer has contacted the inspector responsible for enforcing wage council orders. He has passed on the information to the inspector but requests that he does not contact the firm yet as the negotiations are at a delicate stage. As the Union Officer, how would you use this development? As Chris, when you find out about this new development, how will this affect your intended actions?

Stage 2

1 There has been a failure to reach agreement between Chris and the union official. However, they both are committed to reaching agreement and have concluded some long hours of talking by resolving to take the matter to concil-iation. Chris in particular wished to go to conciliation as he felt it would still leave him more in control of the situation. The two issues that are outstanding are:

(a) the principle of trade union recognition within Mid-Anglia, and

(b) the basic wage rates within the firm and the need to pay the legal minimum wages.

Prepare the written cases to be made to the conciliator by both sides.

2   Enact the meeting between the conciliator, Chris and the union official. Seek to reach agreement on the two issues. Use the procedures of adjournments and separate meetings with the conciliator as part of the proceedings if necessary. Make a written statement on the final outcome of the meeting.

Case 10
Breaking the mould

Analysis

One of the major changes that has taken place in industrial relations in the early 1980s is the shift in power from the traditional shop floor unions towards the management of enterprises. Industrial relations has always been about the balance of industrial power and there are a number of checks and balances within and without the system that result in an equilibrium. The point at which that equilibrium occurs depends on the relative strength of the governing factors. There are many factors but some of the important ones are:

(a) the laws applying to trade union;
(b) the level of employment;
(c) the strength of the order book;
(d) competition;
(e) technology.

The 1980s saw an unprecedented combination that worked to weaken trade unions and to generally strengthen the hand of the employer. In many firms this was seen as the opportunity to introduce radical changes to traditional working practices.

This case is based on a traditional manufacturing company which has a long history but has yet to come to terms with the prevailing climate of the 1980s. Organisations can be very lethargic and only when some external pressure is applied can change be forced on the unwilling structure. With such a static organisation there are often entrenched attitudes and an unwillingness to see what is happening in the world outside. The case is not entirely fictional and is designed to help the reader analyse the problems in such an organisation, to identify the reasons why those problems exist and to suggest how they might be solved.

Background knowledge

In this case you are required to analyse the events in the context of the current industrial, social and economic climate.

Before starting this case you should have some prior knowledge of:

1 The prevailing situation in the 1980s for the factors listed in the introduction above;
2 the meaning of demarcation and restrictive practices and their relationship to productivity;
3 organisational behaviour;
4 traditional trade union functions and behaviour;
5 managing change.

While the case is quite long the comprehensive information is given to portray a picture of the whole organisation rather than a segment. You should use the information as indicators of the organisational culture that exists within the firm and the underlying problems that have never been tackled and the changes that will have to be made.

Introduction

The Northern Electromotor Co Ltd was established in 1905 in the north-west of England. It moved into new premises when it was established and has been using the same site and buildings ever since. The firm makes electric motors for a range of applications from small motors for domestic appliances through to large motors for military and industrial use. The firm has a reputation for making reliable, well-designed motors that have never been low in price but are well made. The firm employs 500 people of whom 350 are in the manufacturing departments and the rest in administration and sales. The company has always been a family firm but the family share-holding in the firm has been declining in recent years as the firm has had to look to outside sources for finance. Nevertheless the family firm atmos-phere still pervades and many employees stay for a long time with the firm; it is not unusual for an employee to stay with the firm for the whole of their working life. The family are still on the board of directors and are held in great respect by employees, albeit sometimes mockingly.

Organisation

The management structure is still a very hierarchical, traditional one with emphasis on lines of authority. In the manufacturing units the structure

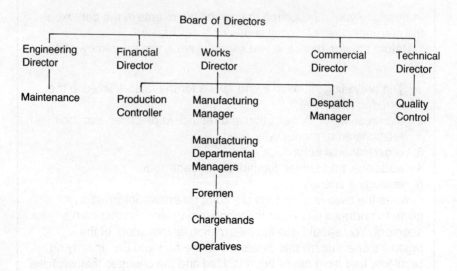

Northern Electromotor Co Ltd

of chargehand and foreman is still prevalent with these characters dominating the work of the sections. A high proportion of the management of the company is people who have risen through the ranks. Usually this means that the foremen and managers are timed-served apprentices who have been with the firm for a long period. Promotion tends very much to be on a seniority basis and those long-serving employees who have been overlooked for promotion have a deep sense of grievance.

There is a grading structure within the firm. In the manufacturing departments this is based on skill and only those with the requisite training are promoted to the higher grades. The lower grades are for the unskilled labourers and they have no chance of reaching the higher grades. In addition the bonus scheme is heavily biased towards the individual's output

Northern Electromotors Co Ltd
Production Operatives-Grading

Level	For		Bonus	Achieved by
Grade 1	lowest	new starters	departmental	unskilled
Grade 2		promoted new starters	departmental	6 months satisfactory performance
Grade 3	middle	new starters/apprentices finishing	individual	apprenticeship
Grade 4		promoted from Grade 3 only	individual	1 year's satisfactory performance
Grade 5	highest	promoted from Grade 4	individual	seniority

and as such only the machine operators (in the higher grade of job) achieve high-bonus payments. The non-operator grades are on a departmental bonus scheme which pays out much less.

In the offices the situation is very much the same as on the shop floor. The clerks tend to be promoted to section leaders and thence to manager on the basis of seniority. There is no bonus scheme in operation in the offices but they have always enjoyed better terms and conditions than the shop floor by trying to maintain the differentials of staff status. This is apparent in the shorter working week and longer holiday entitlement. A grading system operates and this is directly related to pay. The employees are often related to each other and while recruitment has never been through contacts with relations working in the firm, applications from family members has always been encouraged.

Unionisation

The trade union situation in the firm is one of a very strong tradition of trade unionism. This is particularly true on the shop floor and in the maintenance departments. The apprenticeship system is still very strong with the firm still operating an apprentice training workshop through which many employees have come. The union have always taken a keen interest in the number of apprenticeships, ensuring they become card carrying union members. There is a virtual closed shop in that nearly everyone is a union member. Union officials view the production unit as a closed shop and while management have never officially recognised this they have allowed the situation to continue. New recruits are asked to join the union at the interview stage and the personnel department make it clear that they wish to see everyone in the union, if only to keep the peace. When recruits are shown to the department where they are to work the practice has grown for the convenor to see all interviewees. It is recognised that anyone refusing to join the union at that stage has little chance of being offered a job.

The skilled operators are in the Engineering Workers' Union while the labourers are in the General Workers' Union. The latter is less strong because it does not have the numbers nor the structure within the firm to acquire the position that the skilled workers' union has. The fact that few, if any, of the labourer grade workers are ever promoted to the skilled grades means that the general union remains with less power. Anyone promoted to the skilled grades is required to join the skilled, engineers' union.

The situation in the maintenance department is complex. There are five unions in all, with each of the various skill categories having its own union. The fitters are in the engineering union, the electricians in the electrical union, the instrument fitters in another engineering union, the plumbers and pipe fitters in a plumbers union and the trowel trades in yet another union. This has led to many problems over the years, particularly with demarcation difficulties between the various skills, and an almost constant battle with the production departments in ensuring that no maintenance work is carried out by operators or foremen. This includes not even tightening up a loose nut or screw.

The offices are unionised. The only section having staff status that is unionised is the drawing office. This is because of the traditional strong links with the engineers. They are in the draughtsmen's union, not the engineering union of the shop floor. This is to prevent the erosion of staff status that might occur if they were in the shop floor engineering union.

Amongst the clerical staff there is a low level of unionisation and where they have joined, they are in a clerical union. However, several of the office staff, especially those who have joined the firm recently, have been approached by another staff union, whose recruitment policies are aggressive.

The latest move by the second staff union is that it has sent all current clerical union members an application form and some promotional material. This has led to a refusal of any member of the current office staff union to deal with anyone who is a member of the second union and has caused considerable administrative difficulties.

An additional factor of importance, particularly amongst the office staff, is the existence of a staff association. This has maintained itself largely by support from the family directors and is seen as paternalism by many. Its existence has overshadowed the unions in the offices and it is not unknown in some circumstances for managers to use the staff association and its officers as a sounding board rather than the union.

The final category of employee that is unionised is the supervisors. Traditionally they had remained in the same unions as in their previous jobs. However, as the job of the supervisor became more 'managerial' the supervisors, in both the production and maintenance departments, decided to break away and join a staff union. This proved to be an astute move for the supervisors as they benefited from this enormously. They were recognised as a special case and were given good pay rises and better terms and conditions. While this produced a rift with the shop floor unions it generated a great cohesion within the supervisors factory-wide. To some extent this worked in management's favour as it caused the supervisors to become a category on their own, rather than just an extension of the shop floor, where they had come from. The supervisors would not necessarily follow the shop floor on an issue but would decide for themselves.

The current structure of the trade unions at Northern Electromotor is summarised in the table on p. 59.

Industrial relations

Over the years the company had acquiessed or allowed (by turning a blind eye) a number of questionable practices to creep in. The role of collective

Union	Covering	Comments
Engineering Workers' Union	Grades 3, 4, 5. Apprentices	Manufacturing Special category
	Maintenance fitters Fitters' mates	Special category
General Workers' Union	Grades 1 and 2 Despatch Department Drivers	Manufacturing Internal and external transport
Electrical Engineers' Association	Electricians and mates	Including apprentices
Instrument Technicians' Union	Instrument engineers	Including apprentices
Plumbers and Allied Trades Union	Plumbers and pipe fitters	
Builders and Trowel Trades Union	Bricklayers and building repairs	
Association of Draughtsmen	Draughtsmen	
Clerical Workers' Union	Clerical staff, secretaries etc., incl. some junior managers	
Amalgamated Union of Office Workers	Same as above	Acquired by 'poaching'
Society of Managerial Staffs	Production and maintenance supervisors	No managers in this union

bargaining was restricted to the annual round of pay and conditions with the occasional incident being taken up through the official grievance procedure. This meant that few topics were ever negotiated openly or a written agreement made. What had tended to happen was that a practice was 'tried on' and, if allowed to continue, became accepted practice for all time. The role of the full-time convenor was crucial. The engineering union (being the biggest and strongest) had a convenor. He would sometimes act on behalf of the other unions, but only if it suited. There was more bargaining in the convenor's office, and more deals made, than anywhere else. When the managers and directors found out what was happening they would vent their anger but were powerless to do very much unless they were prepared to take the unions on and face a struggle. This did not happen very often though.

Questionable practices

The practice has developed that operators on one section who have little work to do cannot be transferred to another section, even though it might mean operating the same machine. If an operator is working a lathe in the commutator section and has little work, supervision can not transfer the operator to the body section. This could only be achieved through a permanent transfer, which involves a disturbance allowance.

Overtime is allocated by the union officials. The supervisor calculates what extra work is needed. The number of people to come in and for how long is decided as between supervisor and union official. This has always erred on the side of providing more hours than is really necessary. Although there is a rule relating to attendance which states that anyone late twice in one week cannot be offered overtime, this is ignored.

In the maintenance department a fitter has always to be accompanied by another fitter, even though there may be little work for the second man. This is the remains of the practice of the skilled man always having a mate.

In the offices there have been a number of developments recently. The office workers have traditionally been very loyal to the firm, feeling that they work for the family personally. While there has been no expansion in jobs in the offices the impact of modern office machinery has been minimised by the managers allowing natural wastage to take care of any over-staffing. There have never been any redundancies and many feel that they are well looked after.

Overall, the industrial relations record of the firm has not been any worse than that of a company of its size in the engineering sector. It has suffered the occasional strike, the most recent being five years ago when the management reply in pay negotiations was 0 per cent. After a week the management settled on much more favourable terms. Probably the record is a reflection of the slightly soft approach to problems, particularly from the directors, by either hiding them or finding an easy way out. Such an ad hoc policy has led to the situation where the unions are sometimes deliberately provocative to test what the reaction might be.

Current position

While commercially the firm has always done reasonably well it has never produced high levels of profit, nor has it expanded its markets in recent times. Having earned its reputation in the market place it has held its share of the business. From time to time the firm has had to find extra money to finance the replacement of machinery and to modernise plant and office equipment. This has led to a dilution of the family shareholding and to the appointment of directors by the organisations providing this finance. The current crisis is the most serious the firm has suffered in its 80-year history. It has been caused by a number of factors with the order book stagnant, a lack of investment, loss of competitiveness and a rising labour cost problem.

This has led to the shock announcement by the directors that the company has been taken over by an industrial holding group as from the next week. There had been no leaks and no one had any details of the deal.

Later there was a fuller announcement which gave more details about the take-over:

Northern Electromotor Co Ltd
Announcement

Take-over by Acme Industrial Holdings

The Directors wish to announce to its employees some further details of the take-over of the company by the Acme Industrial Holdings Group. The company is now owned by the group and the group are in charge of operations as from last week. The take-over has been imposed upon us out of necessity as the firm has been in a very weak position and still is. We are not gaining sufficient orders to maintain us in business, we are no longer generating profits and our productivity is low. The take-over is not a guarantee of our survival. We have been set some very tight targets to achieve in a short period of time. If these are not achieved Acme, on reviewing the situation, may chose to take drastic action. Had we tried to survive this crisis alone we would have had no alternative but to have closed the firm. Our creditors were not prepared to help us any longer.

Clearly in order to meet the targets set by our new owners, great changes are required in a very short space of time. These are not a matter of choice or negotiation and many of them were a pre-requirement of the take-over. In particular the following changes will be made:

1 All current collective agreements will be honoured but substantial changes will be made to them.

2 Only one union will represent the whole of the workforce.

3 Staff reductions will have to be made, across the board.

4 Current working practices will be reviewed and changes made to increase productivity.

We urge all our employees to co-operate in the measures that we need to take in order to ensure our survival.

Exercises

1 You are employed as an industrial relations officer by the holding group that has taken over Northern Electromotor in their personnel department. You have been tasked with investigating the current industrial relations situation at Northern Electromotors. You have to write a report on the situation, analyse the current strengths and weaknesses within the firm and recommend what changes should be made. Also include a section on how these changes should be introduced. You should examine the stated intention to have only one trade union in the firm.

2 The Engineering Workers' Union have taken up the case of the sudden take-over of Northern Electromotor at national level. Their main complaint is the manner in which the announcement has been made and the complete lack of consultation and deliberate secrecy. They have taken up the issue as an official dispute under the National Agreement. As a researcher in the union's District Office you have been detailed to this dispute. The union's officers require an analytical report on the situation that pertains at Northern Electromotor and have asked for a series of recommendations to be made on what the union ought to do to secure the best possible deal for its members at Northern Electromotors. The report should include a discussion on both tactics and strategy.

3   Convene a meeting between the new employers and the union officials at Northern Electromotor. The object of this meeting is to discuss the demands made by the new employers in their announcement of the take-over with a view to establishing the particular changes that the company is seeking and how they expect to implement these. Run this exercise by allocating roles to the members of your group.

4   You are a Production Manager in one of the manufacturing departments at Northern Electromotor. You have received a memo from the new firm's Personnel Manager which states that all cases of demarcation and restrictive practices should be identified and eradicated.

The first task is to list the instances where you know these to exist. The second step is to produce notes on the way in which you intend to eliminate these practices for a presentation that you are required to give at the next senior manager's meeting.

Case 11

The mushrooming problem

Analysis

Frequently disputes are not straightforward, especially where the dispute is not confined only to one issue. More often the source of a dispute is a mixture of different issues and there is one final incident that precipitates the dispute. The difficulty in resolving these situations is knowing which of the many issues needs solving to restore normal relations. Indeed the major issue may change during the course of the dispute and the original cause may be forgotten altogether! The important lesson to be learnt from these situations is to deal with the issues quickly and decisively as they occur and to invoke procedures as soon as possible to solve them rather than leave the issues to fester. Inevitably problems that are left un-attended become bigger rather than smaller and the minor soon becomes major. The following case relates to a situation in which this has happened and finding a solution may not be easy.

Background knowledge

Many of the everyday actions of managers have some implications for industrial relations. As they perform their various managerial tasks they need to work out what the possible implications are. This is particularly true where managers are concerned with managing change within the organisation. One of the objectives a production manager is constantly trying to achieve is improvements in productivity. This often involves changes in the working practices of employees and hence has important industrial relations implications. This requires managerial skills of a high order. Any mistakes can be very costly.

Before starting this case you should have some prior knowledge of:

1   the basic concepts of organisations, authority and responsibility;
2   the managerial functions of planning, organising, delegating, communicating and controlling;
3   the management of change and what constitutes good practice;
4   the involvement of trade unions and employees in the process of communication and consultation;
5   resolving grievances and disputes quickly and effectively;
6   handling major disputes that have led to or could lead to industrial action.

The Hertford Chemical Co

In its 12-year history the Hertford Chemical Co has built up a reputation as a supplier of chemicals to a range of manufacturers, mainly synthetic resins and bases for other chemical products. This reputation has been built on technical expertise and the ability to supply highly complex chemicals in large quantities. Out of the 120 employees ten are employed purely on development work with others involved in pilot plant work and transferring new formulations to the plant. On the main manufacturing plant there are 32 operatives split between four shifts, each headed by a shift foreman. The plant works seven days a week, 48 weeks a year. The shifts of eight operatives are split between two buildings with each group of four being headed by a Section Leader. The plant consists of a number of reaction vessels and mixing tanks with a complex of pipes, pumps, filters, by-passes, meters and other items of a typical chemical plant. Not all the vessels and tanks are used all the time as many of them are suited only to the production of particular products.

Organisation

The organisation of the plant has grown in rather a haphazard manner with changes being made to suit the prevailing circumstances. The current situation is that the operatives have been trained (in the loose sense of the word) on certain items of plant and they stick to these, almost possessively. The operators and section leaders in the two buildings tend to be separate and, although they are next door to each other, there is little or no transfer of labour between the two. There is some logic to this in that the products are specific to the various items of plant and each operator builds up some expertise in the products made and in the operation of the plant.

For the ancillary operations on the plant, such as raw material delivery, product removal, cleaning and similar duties, there is a day team of six men which carry out these functions during normal working hours (7.30 am to

The Hertford Chemical Co

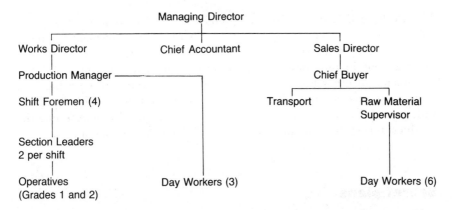

4.30 pm) with a considerable amount of overtime worked to keep the plant serviced and to supplement income. The removal of solid products is wholly performed by a team of three men. They work normal day hours and much overtime during the week and at week-ends. With the unpredictable nature of timing the completion of batches, planning their activities is very difficult. Between off-loading finished product from the plant they help with other ancillary duties.

Collective bargaining

The plant is unionised and while there is not a closed shop some 95 per cent of operatives are in the union. The foremen are in a separate, staff union. Formal procedures are evolving but generally industrial relations are conducted 'by the seat of the pants' with each situation taken as it arises. Annual pay negotiations take place between the union officials and management but little else is negotiated formally. Generally, relations are quite good considering the industry and while the company has been expanding there have been few traumatic experiences.

Pay

The basic pay rates are quite low but earnings are boosted with shift premiums and overtime. With the nature of the shifts everyone does some overtime as the basic working week is 39 hours and the average working week is 42 hours. The day worker's rates are also low but again they boost their earnings with regular overtime, both mid-week and at week-ends. Overtime rates are time and one-third during the week, time and a half Saturday and double time Sunday and statutory holidays.

Conditions

The work itself is dirty and smelly and can involve some hard physical labour, especially when things go wrong. There is also an element of danger as most of the chemicals used are dangerous (some highly poisonous) and the reactions in the vessels are performed at high temperatures and can be violent. At other times it can be boring, for example when a batch of material is mixing, and this may go on for several hours with relatively little to do. The work also involves some technical knowledge in testing the product during manufacture which is carried out by the operatives.

Secret plans

Unknown to the shop floor or their union representatives, the Works Manager had instituted a drive to improve productivity. This included an improvement in labour productivity which he saw as being low due to a number of factors.

Primarily he was looking to change the patterns of working so that there was a greater degree of flexibility as between the operatives on the shifts, especially between the two buildings, and between the day workers and the shift workers. His fear was that if the present work arrangements became too entrenched it would become increasingly difficult to change the patterns of working. He believed the time was right as the firm was going through a not unfamiliar dip in the order book and, while there was no threat to jobs, things needed tightening up to lower unit costs.

The prime target for reducing the wage bill was to reduce overtime payments. The total bill for overtime was very high, added to which it was causing productivity to fall because the marginal cost was high, especially with week-end working.

The Works Manager intended to achieve this through a steady, gradual process of minor changes rather than go for an all out blitz on working practices. Currently he was not revealing his hand to the foremen, although he would have to work through them. He had spoken about his plans to the Managing Director and to the Production Manager. The first step he had taken was to send a message to the foremen asking them to ensure that if there was not sufficient work in one building to occupy all the operatives normally employed there, then they must transfer one (or more) operatives into the other building and put them under the charge of the Section Leader of that building. He asked the foremen to monitor this by checking the signatures on the work sheets, as these would reveal whether any personnel had been transferred. In the event there were two occasions in the first week when a foreman did effect a transfer, although notably it was the same foreman and person on both occasions.

Further edicts

A further step was taken two weeks later. This time the Works Manager asked that where there was spare labour (either because there was no work for that vessel or it was on a long processing time) the operative should be given other duties. These might include loading solid, finished product (normally carried out exclusively by the day workers), loading raw material for another operative who needs some help or other duties that the foreman might specify. Nothing much happened at first and monitoring this stage was more of a problem, as the foremen had still not been informed of the reasons behind the moves, nor their co-operation sought. The Works Manager was reluctant to do this as the foremen still identified themselves with the workforce rather than the management.

Alongside the exercise being carried out in the production unit, the day worker's manager had also been instructed to reduce the levels of overtime worked, both week-days and week-ends. The idea was to reduce the level of planned overtime and to slowly transfer this extra work to the shift men. As the shift men were being paid anyway, and there was no case for their numbers to be reduced, this seemed to be an efficient way of increasing productivity. Added to this there had always been more than a suspicion that 'while the cats were away the mice did play'. Supervising these men outside the normal hours of the day managers had always been a problem. The shift foremen maintained their job was to supervise the plant and its operatives, not anyone else. For example, it was suspected that those booked on overtime would leave early and someone else would clock them out or, alternatively, they would be clocked in early on week-end mornings. Also the rate at which these people worked after normal hours was always commented upon as being exceptionally slow.

Something's afoot

Six weeks after the start of the campaign it was obvious to all that something was happening although no one knew quite what, or they kept it quiet. This created a feeling of unease and the union at its recent, unusually well attended branch meeting, felt that vigilance was required to prevent the terms and conditions of the workforce being worsened by stealth. The shop steward went to see the Works Manager after the meeting but was given the rather bland reply that he was merely doing the job that he had always done and there was nothing to worry about. This did nothing to reassure the men and the union policy adopted was to look out for any changes to current practice and to resist these, even if this meant a refusal to operate a new practice. The union promised to back anyone subject to disciplinary action as a result of this.

The new employee

Labour turnover at the Hertford Chemical Co is relatively high. The nature of the work and the unsocial hours combine to prompt people to leave for more convivial jobs. As a result of this, recruitment occurs quite frequently and often at very short notice. This has lead to a quick hire policy; if they breathe, take them on! Such hasty decisions have seen some people recruited that, on reflection, should not have been taken on.

One person in this category was Stan Jessop. He quickly made his mark on the shift by becoming the loud mouth who made a nuisance of himself to everyone. The foreman noted this after the first shift and had his suspicions confirmed time and again. The moment the position of shop steward fell vacant he virtually elected himself to it. In the event no-one else stood for election, so he was elected unopposed. Secretly the managers were wishing they could fire him but he never quite gave them sufficient grounds to do so, although his standard of work was poor and Stan had high disregard for his foreman or anyone in authority. He had had a verbal warning against him for persistent lateness but played a canny game and waited until the warning was about to be extinguished before reverting to his former bad habits.

The present week-end had been a busy one. Everything that could go wrong, had virtually happened. The foremen had been frantically trying to keep the production programme together and a mixture of absences, breakdowns, lack of raw materials and technical difficuties had all combined to make it one of the worst week-ends possible. The final problem arose on the Sunday night shift. As a result of the problems encountered over the week-end, the production programme had been revamped because certain equipment was no longer available until Monday morning when the engineers came in. This meant that operators had to be moved around to work on the equipment that was running. The shift foreman, after taking over from his colleague at 10.00 pm, decided, in consultation with his Section Leaders, on the allocation of work.

This entailed Stan Jessop being moved from his normal duties to the next building to help them. There was plenty to do and it was agreed that it was best to keep Stan occupied. The foreman approached Stan tactfully and explained the reasons for the request. This was met with a tirade of abuse and invective, the like of which the foreman had never heard before (and he had a good command of the English language). It was clear that Stan would not carry out the request! The foreman then reiterated his instruction and said that, in the event of Stan not doing as requested, the matter would be reported to the Works Manager and would almost certainly lead to disciplinary action. That argument only served to make Stan even more angry and to hurl accusations at the foreman and management of victimisation. The foreman walked away and left Stan to calm down and hopefully, after a time of reflection, go to his work. Unfortunately this did not occur. Stan made a round of the other operators and told them about the occurence. He then returned to the foreman and requested an emergency union meeting, which was refused.

The foreman contacted the Production Manager and asked his advice on what to do. The advice was that in the event of Stan refusing to do the work as instructed he should be sent home, suspended on full pay, and told to report to the Works Manager the following morning. In the meantime, the foreman should write a report on the incident for the Manager to collect in the morning. After receiving this advice the foreman observed that Stan was still wandering round the plant speaking to anyone who would listen and even to those who did not want to listen. He had a cup of tea with him. This was against company rules, as it is illegal (on a chemical plant). He would not leave the plant when requested and he was trying to induce others to drink tea on the plant by bringing cups out to them. The foreman spoke to him firmly and demanded he leave the plant and report back in the morning. Stan said he couldn't do that as he had been given a lift in by a colleague. The foreman said that he would have to stay off the plant all night and could remain in the canteen. Eventually Stan made his way to the canteen and fell asleep. He left at 6.00 am after the foreman reminded him to report in later that morning.

The meeting

Stan eventually came in to see the Works Manager at 2.00 pm. By this time the Manager had been able to ascertain most of the facts relating to the previous night's incident and was ready for Stan. The meeting was very curt and bad tempered. When both men had calmed down there was some discussion on the issues after which the Works Manager said that Stan would be suspended on full pay pending a proper disciplinary hearing. Stan said that it would not be necessary. He could represent himself and wanted the present meeting to resolve the issue one way or the other. The meeting carried on and clearly no headway was being made. Stan stuck to the argument that the foreman had no right to instruct him to do a job he had not been trained for, and it would be a safety risk if nothing else. The Manager said that the foreman's order was legitimate and Stan should have done as asked. There were frequent asides into the incidents of shouting, abuse, tea drinking, lateness, attitudes and so on but this got neither side anywhere. Finally, at 4.30, the Manager said that if Stan was not prepared to consider another meeting to resolve the issue then the only course of action open to him was to dismiss Stan. At that Stan leapt up, stormed out of the room and was away down to the works. As he was unable to persuade the current shift at work to support him he left the site soon after.

The walk out

At 6.00 the next morning, when Stan's shift returned, Stan was in extra early to see all his colleagues. They were asked, by Stan, to come to a brief meeting in the canteen. The foreman said they were not to have such a meeting in work time. This was ignored. The outcome of the brief meeting was that the men said they would walk out in support of Stan and also to protest against the changes that were being made. The Works Manager had come on site extra early, in case there was any trouble, and immediately went in to see the men before they dispersed. After a tense, short meeting the men reaffirmed that they would walk out. The Manager said that obviously he could not forcibly make them stay but pointed out the possible consequences of their actions. This again had no effect. Finally the Manager stated that before walking out the men should go onto the plant to make it safe and to ensure that any reactors currently in-process were not likely to cause a major incident if left unattended (this could well be the case when processing some products). The men did not heed this request and promptly left the site. The foreman contacted the Production Manager and others who were available to come in and assist in closing down the plant.

Fortunately the plant was in a condition whereby it could be closed down with little damage being done. At 1.00 pm the Security Officer of the firm who shared the site with Hertford Chemicals reported a small group of men standing at the bottom of the drive. The Works Manager went to the gatehouse and soon determined that they were the striking men. He walked down to see them and told them that they could reconsider their decision to strike but if they continued to stay out on strike they were not to remain on company property, particularly if they intended to picket the next shift, due on soon. They were told to leave. However, they did not leave as the entrance to the works was on a main road and clearly picketing was not possible there.

Exercises

1 What action should the firm take:
   (a) to stop the picketing;
   (b) to avert the industrial action spreading to the other shifts?

2 Convene a meeting between the Works Manager, the Production Manager, the union District Official and a shop steward from another shift. The meeting should consider how the dispute can be resolved.

   An addition to this exercise could be that the Managing Director has set as a pre-condition to a discussion on the issues, that there is an immediate return to work. This is not negotiable.

3 Prepare a brief for the management side on the strengths and weaknesses of their case. Also present the options open to them, the possible outcomes and the points to which they should stick and those on which they should be flexible.

4 Prepare a similar brief for the union side.

5 Act as the conciliator to whom Stan Jessop's claim for unfair dismissal has been sent.
Prepare to meet the two sides and attempt to conciliate a settlement. Have members of your group take on the role of the other actors in this case. They should present their case to you, as conciliator, and you can decide whether to hold a joint meeting or separate meetings of the two sides. Keep in mind that the conciliator is only investigating the dismissal of Stan Jessop. Prepare a brief report on the outcome of the conciliation.

6 At the request of the Managing Director write a confidential report on the state of industrial relations in the firm. In particular he wishes you to analyse the various incidents of the case.

7 Act an Industrial Tribunal to hear the case of Stan Jessop. (Assume that Stan was finally dismissed.) Role play the actors – Chairperson, employer panel representative, employee panel representative, employer (Hertford Chemical Co manager or solicitor), union official (or solicitor), Stan, his ex-shift foreman, and anyone else needed as a witness. Arrive at a decision and write the promulgation for the case.

8 The Hertford Chemical Co has never employed a personnel officer until now. Partially as a result of this episode, the firm have employed you as their Personnel Officer. Review the existing industrial relations policies and practices, write a report on your findings and make recommendations.

9 After the dispute was resolved the Managing Director set up a small committee including the Works Manager, the Production Manager and the Personnel Officer to investigate and report on the means of achieving changes in working practices at Hertford Chemical Co. Produce a report that analyses the situation and recommends improvements to the system of management.

Case 12

Custom and practice

Analysis

In industrial relations it is often the small issues that become major which lead to a dispute that is difficult to resolve. To an outsider it seems senseless and pointless that the two sides can fail to agree on what appears to be a matter of insignificant detail. However, the parties to the dispute see it as a matter of principle or it is the small issue that finally 'breaks the camel's back' and merely represents a manifestation of the underlying poor state of industrial relations at a firm. This case is not unique in that it deals with the delicate issue of an alleged entitlement (i.e. extended tea breaks) by a group of employees built up over a period of time, and a manager's determination to alter this traditional custom and practice.

Background knowledge

In this case you are required to examine the situation in a small firm where a manager is charged with making radical improvements in the firm's performance. In doing so he challenges some of the practices which the union argue have been established over time and which he counterclaims are in breach of existing agreements. The manner in which the manager tackles the issue helps precipitate a stoppage of work.

Before starting this case you should have some prior knowledge of:

1   the status and application of collective agreements;
2   the effects of custom and practice on these agreements;
3   the management and negotiation of change;
4   the benefits of consultation and agreement.

Introduction

The Romiley Manufacturing Co is an old established firm, the major part of whose production is exported. For some time they have been experiencing difficulty in keeping delivery dates. As a result orders have fallen off despite the advantages of a favourable exchange rate. In an effort to improve matters John Roberts, an outsider with a reputation for efficiency, was engaged six months ago as Works Manager.

Too long tea breaks

Roberts quickly began to tighten up on systems and practices. New systems of production control and quality control were introduced which, coupled with other changes, began to produce results. One aspect to cause Roberts concern was the length of the morning and afternoon tea breaks. These had been agreed in a signed union/management agreement, twelve years ago, at ten minutes, but had gradually increased to twenty. He was not only concerned about the loss of output this represented, and the effect on the firm's major problem of keeping delivery dates, but also because he saw it as a clear indication that supervision was far too easy going. Roberts firmly believed that supervisors should supervise and that agreements should be kept to the letter.

One day all members of supervision were called to a meeting where Roberts informed them of his intentions to have the tea-break agreement observed. He made it clear that supervisors would be held responsible for bringing their own departments into line as quickly as possible.

Having done his job properly, as he saw it, by first putting supervision in the picture, Roberts sent for the Works Convenor, Charlie Wilson and informed him of his intentions. Wilson protested that the tea-break facilities were inadequate, and warned that there would probably be trouble. Roberts replied that the shop stewards had never complained or even mentioned the tea-break facilities to him since he joined the firm. He added that if there were aspects of facilities that needed improvement he would be prepared to discuss them, but only after the men had made every attempt to observe the agreement on the ten minutes.

Simultaneously, at the time of this meeting, notices were posted in the factory informing employees that the agreed ten minutes must be observed and warning that, if necessary, disciplinary action would be taken against offenders.

Shop floor reaction to this notice was immediate. The Works Convenor informed Roberts that unless the notice was withdrawn, there would be a strike. Roberts replied that he was acting within his rights in seeking to apply the agreement and while he hoped it would not be necessary to use disciplinary measures, any action taken would be subject to the agreed

```
┌─────────────────────────────────────────────────────────────────────┐
│                     ROMILEY MANUFACTURING CO                         │
│                                                                       │
│                          N O T I C E                                  │
│                                                                       │
│   FROM:    A Roberts                                  12 March 19--   │
│                                                                       │
│   TO:      All Production Personnel                                   │
│                                                                       │
│   As from today all breaks, morning and afternoon, will be taken in   │
│   accordance with the agreement made with the trade union. This       │
│   specifies that there will be a break in the morning, from 10.20 to  │
│   10.30, and in the afternoon, from 3.20 to 3.30. Any increase in     │
│   the length of these breaks represents a loss in production and in   │
│   personnel breaking the agreements which should be adhered to by     │
│   all parties.                                                        │
│                                                                       │
│   Any personnel not observing the agreed length of break will be      │
│   subject to disciplinary action.                                     │
│                                                                       │
│   A Roberts                                                           │
│                                                                       │
└─────────────────────────────────────────────────────────────────────┘
```

disciplinary procedure. He would not however be party to allowing people to violate agreements, nor be blackmailed into paying them for not working.

The strike took place.

Exercises

1 Having gathered the information relating to this incident, as John Roberts' immediate superior, carry out an appraisal on Roberts handling of the affair. Prepare this as a statement to give to Roberts. At the end ask Roberts to see you regarding the matter.

2 As John Roberts, you have been summoned to your immediate superior. Prepare some notes on the incident, giving your explanation of what you have done and state how you are prepared to see the dispute settled.

3 Role play the meeting between Roberts and his superior.

4 The union have convened a meeting prior to the negotiating committee meeting. As Charlie Wilson state what you see as the important issues in the dispute and explain your approach to the meeting.

5 In a group, act as a negotiating committee convened to resolve the dispute. Each side should prepare their case in advance and the committee should proceed by:
  (a) each side making an opening statement;
  (b) identifying the main issues;
  (c) making proposals that should lead to a settlement.

6   As a variation, the management side can make a pre-condition to the negotiations that there is a return to work. Introduce this to the negotiations in **5**.

7   Assuming that the dispute is not resolved by internal negotiation, either
individually or in groups, set out the statements of claim to be submitted to an
arbitrator by the union side and the management side.

8   Acting as an arbitrator study the statements of claim from each side. Set out
the questions you would ask each side and put forward your proposals for a
settlement.

9   Alternatively, the groups in **5** can act as union and management respectively
and role play the process of conciliation, with one of the group nominated as
conciliator.

10   As a personnel consultant, submit a report on how the firm should handle
similar change situations and how it should proceed with any further changes
it wishes to make.

Case 13
The high-risk driver

Analysis

Usually when management are dealing with questions of discipline it is for the firm to set standards for itself and to institute a system of enforcing those rules. In some industries there are legal constraints and standards set which have to be taken into account. There are occasions when a third party will intervene in the running of a business and create a problem involving discipline. This case illustrates a situation in which a constraint is imposed on a firm and they have to act severely to deal with a situation they should have dealt with a long time ago.

Background knowledge

In this case you are required to examine a rather delicate situation in which a firm is forced, not through its own making, to take action against one of its own employees or face the possible prospect of not being able to continue in business.

Before starting this case you should have some prior knowledge of:

1 disciplinary procedures;
2 disciplinary action;
3 unfair dismissal law;
4 the human relations skills of handling people in difficult and delicate situations.

Introduction

Bill Watson is a heavy goods vehicle driver for a firm that supplies fresh fruit and vegetables around the West country. He has been a driver for the firm since he left the army in 1956 in which he had a job as a driver. Bill is a steady employee and the firm has never had any major disciplinary problems with him during his 30 years with the firm. Currently Bill drives a large articulated lorry and has regular runs into the London markets and delivery points in Devon and Cornwall. He enjoys his job, in that it gets him out and about, but recently he has been feeling that he does not like the heavy traffic nor the tendency within the industry towards heavier lorries. He can remember the days when the roads were much quieter and life was not as rushed, which he repeats frequently to anyone who will listen to his reminiscences.

The high-risk driver

The state of Bill's nerves and the dislike of the pressures of road haulage have partially been generated by a series of accidents in recent years. His first major accident occurred during stormy weather one spring some seven years ago. He was driving down to London with an empty, high sided lorry when he was blown off the road into a ditch. Fortunately Bill was not injured, except for suffering from shock. The lorry was extensively damaged and the insurance company had a large bill to pay. The Transport Manager had advised Bill that if the weather turned too stormy he must stop and await calmer weather. Bill thought he knew better than the Manager, added to which he wanted to be back that night for an evening out he had arranged.

This accident was to prove to be the first of a long series of accidents, many minor and a few major. There were a number of minor incidents such as backing into other vehicles. In one recent incident, involving backing into a stationary, unoccupied car, Bill drove away without reporting the accident, although he knew he had damaged the car. The owners were told of the accident and Bill's firm were contacted and had to process a claim through their insurance company. Fortunately for Bill, the police were not informed and there were no legal proceedings taken. This was due to the placatory moves made by the Transport Manager to calm the stormy waters. He didn't want a public court case that could damage the reputation of the firm. Again, luckily for Bill, the firm did not institute any formal disciplinary action against Bill although he was formally told that such incidents must never occur again.

Accident proneness

The last two years had seen no improvement in Bill's accident record. In this period he had caused damage to his own and other vehicles on seven occasions. The Transport Manager was getting very cautious about letting Bill on the road but there was no other job for Bill to do except drive and there was nothing else that Bill wanted to do except drive. The firm did not have any light goods vehicles so there was no opportunity to put Bill on lighter work. Few of the accidents could be put down wholly to Bill's negligence and he seemed to have learnt his lesson regarding reporting accidents. The firm were concerned about the rising insurance costs because they had lost their no claims bonuses and were currently being penalised for having such a bad claims record.

The annual renewal notice for the firm's vehicle insurance arrived last week. The covering letter was not the usual computer processed, personalised letter but a long letter from the Regional Manager of the company:

MENDIP INSURANCE COMPANY

76 Severn Street, Barton

23 September 19--

Managing Director
West Country Haulage Co
Ciderworks Lane
Bridgeford

Dear Sir

As you are aware, the insurance for your fleet is due for renewal on
1st October. We have reviewed your insurance contract with us and
there is a matter which I have to raise with you. Over a period of
years, there has been a relatively large number of claims made which
have resulted in our paying out considerable sums of money to settle
these. Having analysed the details of the claims we find that the
majority are due to one driver, Mr W Watson. I append a list of these
for you.

It is noticeable that the premium we have had to charge over the years
has increased considerably due to loss of no claims discount and a
loading for the high rate of accident claim. We have concluded that we
can no longer issue insurance cover for your vehicles under the present
arrangements. We would consider issuing cover providing that Mr W Watson
was no longer a driver, as we now consider him to be an uninsurable risk
due to his accident proneness.

Please contact me at this office if you wish to discuss possible insurance
arrangements.

Yours faithfully

G Shepherd.

G Shepherd
Regional Manager

Loss of insurance?

The letter caused a flurry of activity. The insurance company had not been fair as they had only sent the letter one week before the renewal date. Clearly the firm would have to act, and quickly. A telephone conversation with the Regional Manager, who had sent the letter, only served to confirm the position. The insurance company would not compromise at all and furthermore the ban on Bill included all vehicles, not just the articulated lorries Bill currently drove. A telephone conversation with a local insurance broker elicited the information that no other insurance company would issue a policy without checking with the previous insurers of the firm. This would reveal the problem regarding a certain driver and then that firm would refuse to issue a policy except at a very high, prohibitive premium. It would also invalidate any future insurance policy if they failed to declare the fact that another insurance company had refused to issue a policy to the firm.

The Transport Manager consulted with the Managing Director, who also owned the firm. It was decided to confront Bill with the situation and tell him that the firm had little option but to dismiss him. The Transport Manager was tasked with interviewing Bill and ensuring that he was dismissed so that the insurance company could be informed immediately and the insurance cover needed for next week would not be jeopardised.

The Transport Manager telephoned Bill that night and asked him to come to his office the next morning and not take the load he was due to take out early the next morning. The Manager did not tell him the reason for the meeting and Bill had an uneasy night trying to guess the reason for it.

Parting company

The meeting took place the next day in a very tense atmosphere. The two men had known each other all their lives. Bill was shown the letter from the insurance company. He asked why he had not been told about the problem before and the fact that there had been a premium paid by the firm for the number of accidents. The Manager was not able to offer Bill any alternative employment and Bill didn't pursue the possibility. Bill was shocked and unable to take in the situation. Finally the Manager told Bill that he would be dismissed from his job as driver from that day and the firm were willing to offer Bill a small, ex-gratia, severance payment over and above his pay in-lieu of notice. This, the Manager hoped, would prevent any unpleasant feelings and would deter Bill from claiming anything further elsewhere (not specifying an Industrial Tribunal, in case it gave Bill any ideas). Bill left the office after the short but tense interview and went home. The Manager wrote a letter confirming the outcome of the

---

WEST COUNTRY HAULAGE

25 September 19--

Mr W Watson
12 Mill Lane
Bridgeford

Dear Mr Watson

I am writing to confirm the outcome of our meeting today and to enclose a cheque for the monies due to you. It is clearly no longer possible for us to employ you as a driver and there is no alternative employment that you will take with us.

We ask that you acknowledge the receipt of this money and that it is accepted on the basis of a full and final settlement, precluding any future claims relating to the termination of your employment with this firm.

On a personal level, I wish to say how sad it is that you have to leave the firm under these circumstances after being with us for such a long time. I wish you all the best for the future.

Yours sincerely

P Stevens

P Stevens
Transport Manager

---

meeting and got the accountant to sign a cheque for the amount due. Bill received the letter and money the next day.

Exercises

1 Role play the meeting between Bill and the Transport Manager where Bill is to be dismissed.

2 Examine the letter sent by the Transport Manager to Bill and assess it, particularly with respect to it being a formal notice of dismissal. Draft a letter that should have been sent based on how you think the case should have been handled.

3 As an advisor to Bill, advice him on whether he should pursue a claim for unfair dismissal. State the possible grounds for the claim and the evidence you would use in a hearing. Obtain and fill in form III (originating application).

4 A Conciliation Officer has been sent to the firm to seek a settlement of Bill's claim for unfair dismissal.

(a) Draft a statement from Bill to the officer or the originating application.

(b) Draft a statement from the firm to the officer or the statement of appearance.

(c) Role play the meeting between the Conciliation Officer and Bill.

(d) Role play the meeting between the Conciliation Officer and the Transport Manager.

(e) State the recommendations that you would make as a Conciliation Officer in this case.

5 Role play the tribunal proceedings that may arise from this incident. Prior to the hearing both sides should prepare their respective cases. This should include an originating application from Bill and a reply from the firm. There should be a panel of three – chairperson, employer representative and employee representative, Bill, his representative, the Transport Manager and a company solicitor. Hear the evidence from both sides, examine and cross examine and finally the panel should promulgate a decision.

6 Advise the Transport Manager on how he should have handled the whole incident. What lessons can be learnt from this case and how should the firm handle such incidents in the future? Advise on the changes the firm should make. In particular, compare the action taken by the firm against the requirements laid down by the Code of Practice on Disciplinary Practice and Procedures in Employment.

7 Prepare a discussion document on how firms should handle the contravention of health and safety rules by employees and the aspect of the possibility of an employee being 'accident-prone'. Draft a typical rule regarding the observance of health and safety rules and the possible consequences of not observing such rules. Suggest how the firm should communicate such a rule and what the broader implications are in specifying such a rule.

Case 14

Temper! Temper!

Analysis

One of the functions of management is to employ competent staff that can cope adequately with the job they are employed to perform. Problems arise when it is clear that an employee is not competent and the work of the organisation is suffering as a result. Such people are often held in derision and they lack any authority or credibility. Management then have to decide what to do. Ultimately incompetence is a fair reason for dismissal but the situation has to be handled fairly. The employee needs to be made aware of their weaknesses and be told where improvement is necessary. The employee must be given time to improve and the support and help that may be required. The situation is even trickier when the person concerned is a member of management. This case, based on a tribunal case, illustrates this point.

Background knowledge

This case deals with a common problem facing many organisations of how to get the best performance from employees and what to do if their performance is not acceptable. The case is not merely about discipline, although that is part of the exercise. It is about how to handle people and how to get the best out of employees.
Organisations have a duty to support their employees and encourage them. This is all the more crucial when the employee concerned is a member of management.

Before starting this case you should have some prior knowledge of:

1   recognising and identifying problems relating to the ability of staff performing their jobs to an acceptable standard and acting to effect an improvement'
2   handling these situations and giving the necessary support;
3   disciplinary procedures and action;
4   human relations; individual and group behaviour;
5   unfair dismissal and constructive dismissal.

Introduction

Every Thursday morning the managers at the headquarters of Auto Silencer Services meet to discuss various routine matters. The meeting is quite formal and a secretary takes minutes and subsequently issues a report of the meeting, noting agreed action etc. About 15 managers meet, including at least one director.

Explosion

The meeting planned for the Thursday in question was a routine one, with no unusual items likely to arise. Stephanie King, manager of the Administrative Support Unit was in attendance as usual. The meeting followed its normal path and was about to finish at 11.00 pm when the Company Secretary, Alan Carter, interjected with an item. He immediately plunged into what could only be described as a tirade of criticism aimed personally at Ms King. He stated that the administrative staff were poorly managed and that he was deeply concerned that the company could no longer carry on without a radical change within the Unit. The blame, he said, lay wholly and completely with Ms King and if she could not cope with the job of Unit Manager then the company would have to think about her future with the firm. Mr Carter gave one or two examples of blunders that had occurred and spelt out the consequences of these in graphic terms. Finally, he said that he had to bring this up at the meeting because that morning two of the staff from Ms King's Unit had been to see him. The jist of their complaint was that they were no longer able to work in the Unit because of the bad feeling, back biting, bickering and lack of discipline in the Unit. When pressed by Alan Carter to elucidate the two said that there had been a vote of no confidence in Ms King and it was a matter of 'she goes or we go'.

This attack on Ms King was entirely without precedent and out of character for the meeting to even raise such questions. The meeting was stunned into silence and nobody tried to stop Alan Carter. Eventually Ms King, desperately trying to maintain her composure, left the room. After the incident there were murmurings that it was not before time and that someone was bound to have said something sooner or later.

Aftermath

Later that day Ms King delivered a short, rather pungent note to the Company Secretary. She did not turn up for work the next day but sent a curt message that she felt ill and would be away (see p. 84).

That same Friday Alan Carter had a meeting with the Personnel Director. They discussed the situation relating to Ms King. They decided that the attack on Ms King had been somewhat unwarranted and the matter had not been handled as it should have been. There was some fric-

20 March 19--

Company Secretary
Auto Silencer Services
Broad Street
Darston

Dear Mr Carter

After the meeting this morning at which you carried out a most
pernicious attack on me personally, I am writing to resign my
position at Auto Silencer with effect from today. You have made
it clear that you no longer consider me competent and have no
faith in me performing the job adequately. Needless to say, I
am most upset at the occurence, what was said and the way you
handled the situation. I would have thought that after 18 years
of loyal service I was due better treatment.

I would be grateful if you would calculate the earnings due to
me and forward them to me.

Yours sincerely

S King

S King

tion between the two because there had been no prior consultation on what
ought to be done about the situation. Ms King was regarded as an expert
on the new office technology and finding a replacement would be difficult.
Clearly her problems were staff management ones but not technical.

The outcome was that a letter was written to Ms King (see opposite).

Return to work

The following Monday, after receiving the letter, Ms King returned to work
and tried to carry on as normal. Nothing was said to her directly but the
atmosphere was strained and unnatural. Things gradually returned to their
previous position and the department settled down. Ms King resolved to
try much harder with her relationships within the department and was
cautious not to be seen to be victimising anyone whom she suspected had
caused the trouble. After the six week period mentioned in the letter she
tried to book an appointment with Alan Carter and was told by his
secretary that she would try to get a meeting arranged but that Mr Carter
was very busy at that time as it was the financial year end. Ms King
contacted the personnel department to arrange an appointment to see the
Personnel Director. She was told that he was away on a course for the next
month.

On the Thursday of that week Ms King was unable to attend the weekly
meeting and sent a deputy in her place. Alan Carter took the opportunity
to quiz the deputy on how things were in the Administrative Support Unit.

```
                    AUTO SILENCER SERVICES

                     Broad Street, Darston




25 March 19--


Ms S King
20 Pintail Avenue
Darston


Dear Ms King

We are in receipt of your letter of 20 March and we have discussed the
situation regarding your continued employment with us.  We accept that
in part we are to blame for the difficulties and we are not prepared
to accept your resignation.

However, we believe that there are some matters which we need to discuss
with you regarding your performance in the job.  Overall, we are satisfied
with the work you produce.  The main criticism made related to your handling
of staff and we will be looking for an improvement in this area.  If there
is any way in which we can help we will be most willing to provide this.
We wish to monitor your progress in this area in the future, and will review
the situation after six weeks.

Would you please contact us at your earliest opportunity so you can start
back with us as soon as possible.  Look forward to seeing you soon.

Yours sincerely


A. Carter

A Carter
Company Secretary
```

He was told that things had not improved and if anything matters were getting worse. Several staff felt that they would be unable to continue to work in the Unit if Ms King remained in post. She was still verbally insulting to staff, short tempered if things went wrong, unable to explain the technicalities of the equipment to others and generally made life unbearable. The members of the meeting murmured that Ms King was clearly unable to supervise and there was an air of resignation that things were unlikely to improve. No decision was taken as the meeting did not handle such matters.

Head office was always a busy place but was currently under extreme pressure due to the need to produce the annual report. The Administrative Services Unit supplied much of the information for the report and hence felt the pressure. Ms King in particular set very high standards and felt that she had to produce the necessary information accurately and quickly. If this did not happen she tended to berate her staff and often lost her temper. The next Monday morning proved to be the final straw. An office junior, who had been with the company for only a short time, was processing some information on a word processor and pressed the wrong key. This cleared all the information from the computer which was needed urgently for another document. It was impossible for the staff to cover for this mistake even by rallying round and doing the work before Ms King found out.

Frayed tempers

When Ms King found out she lost her temper. The young office worker was rounded on for being incompetent and for having wasted so much time. Before long the girl burst into tears but this did not stop the tirade from Ms King. One of the older ladies in the office approached Ms King and exorted her to stop shouting and allow the girl to leave and recover. This had the effect of making Ms King more angry and the older lady was told to get out of the office and stop interfering. Within one minute the whole office was empty and a delegation went to see Alan Carter. The rest of the employees from the Administrative Section went to the canteen.

Having realised that she had gone too far and there was no way she could continue with the firm, Ms King swiftly wrote a letter of resignation and left it in the internal mail tray (see below). She then left by a rear exit and went home.

When the letter of resignation reached the Company Secretary he immediately wrote to Ms King to accept her resignation and to say that

AUTO SILENCER SERVICES
Broad Street, Darston

MEMORANDUM

TO: A Carter

FROM: S King   DATE: 13 May 19—

After the incident that occurred this morning I am resigning my position with the firm as from now. I feel I have been badly treated by you and the firm and obviously matters have not improved, no thanks to your lack of support. Please let me have any monies due to me as soon as possible.

S̶King

S King

her entitlements would be calculated and sent directly to her bank. This placated the still-angry employees from the Unit and they returned to work.

One week later the Managing Director received a formal letter from Ms

---

20 May 19--

Company Secretary
Auto Silencer Services
Broad Street
Darston

Dear Sir

Subsequent to my note of resignation and your reply accepting my
resignation, I am writing to inform you that I have taken legal
advice and have been advised that I have a case to claim constructive
dismissal. You will be receiving a formal notification from the
Industrial Tribunals.

The basis of my claim is that the firm did not give me sufficient
support in my duties and whilst certain problems had been highlighted,
nothing was done to help me. I was promised support but none was
forthcoming and even the review that was promised did not take place
because everyone was too busy. This made the situation completely
untenable and I felt I had to leave.

I am still awaiting the monies due to me and would ask that these are
forwarded immediately.

Yours sincerely

S King

S King

King outlining that she had taken legal advice and was claiming constructive dismissal (see above).

Exercises

1 Write a letter from the Managing Director in reply to Ms King's letter.

2 As Ms King's legal advisor, set out what she will have to do next to pursue
her claim, given that the firm is not prepared to settle out of court. Assess the
strength of her case and what evidence would be needed to prove her case.

3 Assuming that the claim is being taken to a tribunal hearing, as Personnel
Director prepare the case on behalf of the firm. What would be the grounds for
defence? What evidence would you collect and use?

4 Acting as the tribunal chairperson, using the information from Exercises **2** and
3, or by providing your own, decide the case. Write a promulgation for the case,
giving the reasons for your decision.

5 As a Personnel Officer you have been tasked with producing a report on the
incident for the next management meeting. Analyse the possible mistakes that
the firm made in handling this situation. Suggest what the firm should have done
to prevent the situation developing as it did. What changes would you recommend that the firm make to their systems to improve the situation, with particular
reference to personnel policies.

Case 15

Strangers at work

Analysis

A problem that has always existed with the operation of the closed shop is that of the person or group who, because of their beliefs, refuse to join a union. The problem can become intractable because each side sticks to a point of principle. The union believes in the principle of unity and solidarity and the objectors in the principle of their (frequently religious) beliefs and individual freedom. This case examines the situation where there is a racial group which, because of its beliefs, objects to joining a union. Added to this there is the difficulty that arises in a multi-racial workforce where the cultural differences which exist between groups can lead to problems. It also raises the question of the role of management in these delicate situations, where they are not a party to the grievance but are affected by it.

Background knowledge

This case examines two areas of industrial relations that are fraught with danger and difficulty – the closed shop and racial discrimination. These two areas touch on the fundamental aspects of relations in the workplace both in terms of the individual and the group. Because of the nature of these topics any problems that arise are frequently very difficult to resolve as both sides have very strong views on them, often backed by strong principles. Nevertheless, with careful handling such situations can be successfully resolved to everyone's satisfaction.

Before starting this case you should have some prior knowledge of:

1   the formation and operation of a closed shop;
2   the legal aspects of the closed shop and its relationship to unfair dismissal;
3   racial discrimination at work (direct and indirect);
4   the procedures to deal with claims for a closed shop;
5   the skills necessary to handle sensitive situations;
6   the Code of Practice for the Elimination of Racial Discrimination.

The company

The Metal Fastener Group is a West Midlands based firm that manufactures a range of fasteners such as specialist nuts, bolts, rivets, washers and screws. It is a typical firm for the area, employing 150 people of various ethnic origins. The firm has been very open in its recruitment of these groups and has enjoyed good relations with the ethnic communities both in the firm and outside. There has been little trouble in the firm as a result of employing quite a large number of Asians. The Personnel Officer has made particular efforts to ensure that this has been the case. As is often the case, communications have been given especial attention to the extent that some company documents are available to the Asians in their mother tongue. On the face of it, relations between work groups have been reasonable but the Asians workers have preferred to stay with each other rather than integrate. This has meant that the work groups are often all-Asian or all-white. This has not offended anyone and operations have not been affected.

The company's trading position is quite healthy but there is little potential for expansion. The industry is not expanding and the firm has to work on retaining its customers in the face of growing competition. So far there have not been any redundancies but some positions have been left vacant and some natural wastage has occurred. In order to maintain its competitiveness the firm has instituted a number of cost cutting exercises. This has included an examination of labour costs. One way in which the firm has kept these costs down is by employing immigrant workers at wage rates that are considered to be low for the area, though not for the trade. Other local firms, especially in other trades, are able to offer higher wages and some skilled labour has been lost because of this.

Trade union membership

As with most metal fabrication organisations, trade unionism in the firm is strong. The Engineering Union has traditionally recruited in the firm and the level of union membership has been around 60 per cent on the shop floor. In recent times there has been a slight fall in this proportion. Recently, in moves to expand union membership, the union centrally has instituted a campaign for closed shops or 100 per cent membership. The union committee at Metal Fasteners is currently strong and wishes to respond positively to the policy statements of the union. Being aware of the possibility of the need for union protection in what may be difficult times ahead, the union officers within the firm have started a recruitment drive. This has yielded results and the level of membership has risen. Having seen the results of this, a recent branch meeting passed a motion to seek a closed shop agreement for the production departments.

The Asian workers have been approached and, after a discussion on the meaning of a closed shop, the group as a whole have refused to join the union. This has led to a number of informal discussions with the Asians but no headway has been made. The Asians have taken the matter up with their leaders in the community and they have been advised that it would be against their religion to join a union. At the present time the subject has become a source of friction and neither side is openly discussing the issue.

In order to maintain the momentum of the recruitment drive, and in spite of the Asians' refusal to join, the union have had a meeting with management at which they have officially requested a closed shop. Management asked if the union officials knew what the position of the Asian workers was with respect to joining a trade union. They said that the Asians had been approached and there had been a refusal but this did not in any way constitute a block to the union's proposal being made and implemented. The union said that the Asians were a part of the workforce and there was no objection to their presence but the union wished to pursue a policy of 100 per cent membership through the closed shop. However, both sides admitted that the refusal of the Asians to join a union was a problem that needed to be solved. The overall response of the management to the proposal of a closed shop was lukewarm as they did not see the necessity of a formal union membership agreement when the level of union membership was already very high. The firm has always actively encouraged union membership and has given the union a free hand in its recruitment activities. The union's closing statement was that they intended to pursue the matter of the closed shop with vigour and were not prepared to renege on the principles involved, namely full union membership.

The problem grows

The managers in the production departments took some informal soundings amongst the Asian groups. The story they were told was somewhat different to the one they had heard at the meeting. The Asians related stories of harassment and pressure, especially upon the younger Asians. They were concerned that they were being pressurised and had come to the conclusion that the closed shop was a means that the 'white' workers were employing to get rid of the Asian workers and to replace them with non-Asians. This seemed to be the case now that unemployment was a problem in the area. When challenged on why they had not raised this with the managers or supervision, the Asians said they did not think they would be given a fair hearing from the managers who were all white.

At the next union/management meeting the issue of the closed shop was raised and the managers gave evidence of the undue pressure they felt was being put on the Asians. There was concern that the good relations that the firm had had with the Asian community were being harmed and that they could not afford to lose 24 trained workers just for the sake of a closed shop. The union replied that they had not officially sanctioned or even suggested any action against the Asians. They wished that the matter be resolved through the channels of negotiation. However, they were not prepared to retract their claim for a closed shop and wished to press the claim.

The District Officer of the union had been contacted and he supported their claim for a closed shop. He was concerned though that the issue of the Asians refusing to join did not become a matter for media attention as this would lead to bad publicity for the union. The reports of the pressure, particularly the harassment, was not helpful to the union's cause and could lead to the closed shop issue being lost.

The problem finally explodes

The matter was never to be resolved in an orderly manner. The day after the union/management meeting an Asian was told by one of the protagonists for the closed shop (but not a union official) to go to the stores for a 'long weight'. The Asian, after being told by the storekeeper to await the item, returned to the shop floor after one hour. His foreman, not knowing what was going on, reprimanded the Asian and warned him that to leave the shop floor for such a long time without permission could lead to disciplinary action. The Asian immediately saw this as yet another act to get rid of his people from the firm. The irate Asian went up to the person who had sent him to the stores and started to row with him. The consequence was that there was a brawl in which blows were exchanged. The fight was broken up and both men were taken to the Works Manager's office.

Exercises

1 What action should the Works Manager take against the two men who had been fighting?

2 As the Works Manager, make a report to the Managing Director on your recommendations on the outstanding issue of the closed shop, giving the reasons for your recommendations.

3 If you were the Personnel Officer referred to, what would your recommendations be in terms of:
    (a) the closed shop request;
    (b) restoring and improving race relations within the firm;
    (c) the disciplinary action against the two men.

4 The District Officer is informed of the incident and that one of his members

is to be disciplined as a result. What advice would you give to the local union officials at the Metal Fastener Group:
  (a) regarding the claim for a closed shop;
  (b) to improve relations between the union and the Asians;
  (c) regarding the disciplinary action.

5   Discuss the manner in which the firm handled the situation, particularly with respect to race relations. What are the good points, the areas in which improvements could be made and the means that could have been employed to have avoided the incident. Do you have any recommendations for a practicable compromise to resolve the problems at the firm?

6   Assuming the role of a Community Relations/Race Relations Officer, specify the steps that should be taken at the firm, after the incident, to improve race relations. How would you recommend the closed shop issue be resolved?

7   As the leader on the local Asian community, whose advice was previously sought, what advice would you give to:
  (a) the Asians at the firm;
  (b) the Asian involved in the fight;
  (c) what recommendations would you give to restore relations at Metal Fasteners?

8   Role play the disciplinary meeting between the white worker, the Works Manager, the Personnel Officer, the shop steward and the union District Official.

9   Role play the disciplinary meeting between the Asian, the Works Manager, the Personnel Officer and the Asian's community leader.

10   Role play the next union/management meeting convened to discuss the issue of the closed shop. You could include someone role playing the leader of the Asian workers.

11   As a race relations advisor, compile a report on the extent to which both the firm and the union have complied with the detailed requirements of the Code of Practice for the Elimination of Racial Discrimination and the Promotion of Equality of Opportunity in Employment. Where you find bad practice, make recommendations for improving or eliminating it.
  Also examine the question of whether the requirement for union membership in a closed shop might, in this situation, be indirect racial discrimination.

12   Use the Union Membership Agreement form Case 7, and apply it to this case. Use the information about the Metal Fastener Group and apply the agreement at the point prior to the incident of violence. Convene a negotiating committee to conclude an agreement on the form (if any) of a closed shop at the Metal Fastener Group.

Case 16

The unsuitable shop steward

Analysis

One of the features of collective bargaining is that a group of employees are represented by a person of their choice who will act on their behalf in discussions and negotiations with management. That person is variously called shop steward, father/mother of the chapel, corresponding member, work's representative or staff representative. Their function is the same; to be in contact with their members, to represent their members' views and to secure the best deal for them. The manner in which the shop steward is appointed is a matter exclusively for the union. The rules are laid down in the union rule book or in the branch rule book. Providing these are observed then usually the person so appointed is the representative. The usual procedure is that after the person has been appointed a note is sent to the relevant manager for recognition by the organisation. In some firms this will involve issuing credentials, which lays down the basic rights and duties of the shop steward. It is rare for the management of a firm to refuse to issue such credentials or refuse to recognise a duly elected official. When they do refuse, it has to be for an extremely good reason otherwise there will almost certainly be a dispute. Such action is seen as interfering in the internal affairs of the union. This case illustrates a situation in which a shop steward's appointment was not accepted.

Background knowledge

In this case you will be examining the background and run-up to the election of a shop steward and the circumstances under which the management of a firm see fit to challenge the appointment of the steward. The whole situation is a very delicate one which requires industrial relations skills of a high order.

Before starting this case you should have some prior knowledge of:

1 the selection, election and notification of union officials;
2 the independence of trade unions;
3 a typical set of union rules regarding the appointment of lay officials;
4 the recognition and issuing of credentials to a union official;
5 the possible grounds for refusing recognition of a union official;
6 recruitment and selection procedures.

The candidate

Bill Johnson had been a union man all his life. This was not surprising as his father had been a London docker and active in the union in the docks. There was a tradition in the Johnson family to 'get involved' in both trade unions and local politics. Bill had followed his father into the docks but this did not last long due to the decline in the industry. After he left the docks, Bill had a number of jobs in industry as a machine operator. He left the London area when work was getting hard to find and decided to live in one of the London overspill towns that were built in the 1960s. He never stayed long in a firm but always became involved in the union activities and quite often- held union office. It was not unusual for him to become a union official, as in many firms, finding someone willing to take on a union job was not easy, particularly amongst the local people, as they did not have a tradition of trade unionism.

Four months ago Bill started a job at Kingston Plastics as a machine operator. He immediately joined the shop floor union, the General Workers' Union, and started to attend union meetings, where he was vocal from the start. Being familiar with union procedures he impressed his colleagues with his enthusiasm and energy. Two months after Bill joined Kingston Plastics the shop steward elections were due. The current steward for Bill's group had stood reluctantly the year before and had always said that he would only stay on in the post until there was a more willing volunteer. The current steward made the point at a recent branch committee meeting about the impending elections that there appeared to be a more able and willing person than himself available for the post and he would stand down at the end of his term.

Subsequently, when nominations were requested, Bill's name was put forward. He was the only candidate for the section he worked in. Subsequently he was appointed as shop steward for the group; elected un-opposed. The branch secretary then sent the list of the duly elected union officials to the Production Director in the usual way. The next step usually was that the Director replied officially, stating that the company recognised the named individuals as the union representatives for the particular groups.

The unacceptable nomination

The union were not anticipating anything different in this instance. The reply was not always received by return but the first indication of a problem this time was that a reply was taking longer than usual. After an undue delay a note arrived from the Director saying that 'the following were recognised by the company as the recognised union representatives . . .'. Notably the name of Bill Johnson was missing.

The reason for the delay in reply was not because the Director had been dilatory. Quite the reverse. Having received the note from the branch secretary, which contained Bill Johnson's name, he decided that Bill's situation would have to be investigated. Since his appointment there had been concern about him. Initially this was not based on any of his union activities, as management were always careful not to interfere in their business. Soon after Bill's appointment the shift supervisor commented to his manager that he 'had picked a right one this time'. Bill was an extrovert and not slow to make his presence known. A few days after starting he was criticising the firm, its bad management, the poor industrial relations and making comments that he would soon 'sort all that out'.

The recruitment procedure at Kingston Plastics was through advertisement in the local press, application form and interview by the Production Manager. Rarely were references taken up as there was always pressure to get people started as soon as possible and taking up references was always time consuming. In Bill Johnson's case there was no reason, on the face of the application form or interview, to take up any references as everything appeared normal and in order.

Past history revealed

When Bill's name appeared on the union officials' list, his application form was taken out of the file. It revealed no inconsistency but the Production Director requested the Personnel Officer to seek references from Bill's previous employers, but to do this sensitively as suspicions may be aroused. The replies confirmed suspicions. He had a very different track record than the one on the application form. One firm had sacked him almost straight away but Bill had put them down as employing him for two years. The job titles he gave were also erroneous. Seeking further clarification, and hoping to elicit information that Bill's previous employers would not put on paper, the Production Director made contact with them by telephone. Again, the firms that were prepared to talk confirmed the stories and they expanded on Bill's activities, particularly his union activities. The fact that other firms felt they could not give any further information indicated that they had had a problem on their hands but were reluctant to elucidate.

The senior managers decided that, until the position became clearer, they must oppose the appointment of Bill Johnson as shop steward. They could foresee disruption and that was the last thing they wanted. The difficulty was finding a way of doing this without raising accusations of victimisation. The possible grounds for not accepting his appointment were first that it did not comply with the union's rules and second it did not comply with previous custom and practice in the firm. They felt that both arguments were a possibility and they would pursue both lines to try and make a watertight case.

On the question of non-compliance with the union rules, the firm needed to tread very warily, as any investigation of this aspect might arouse suspicions and precipitate an early dispute. The appointment's procedure itself was not against union rules. There was the question of Bill's eligibility, whether he had been a bona-fide member of the union for the requisite period. The union rule book stated that for a person to be nominated as a union official they should have been a fully paid up member of the relevant section of the union for a minimum of one year. The managers did not know which union Bill had been a member of at his last place of work although they had ascertained that there had been a gap of two months in his employment between his last job and his appointment at Kingston Plastics.

On the second question, of custom and practice, they felt they could make a case that it was highly improbable that a person that had only been with the firm two months at the time of the nomination could know sufficient about the firm, its employees and its procedures to make a sensible contribution and act as a representative. Normally they would look to a nominee having been with the firm for two years. Looking back at the records the managers found that no one had been appointed to a union post with less than two years service. This seemed to strengthen their hand in this argument.

Trouble brewing

The pace started to hot up as soon as the note from the Production Director was received by the union secretary. The District Official was contacted and he met the branch chairperson and secretary the same day, but the information was not disclosed to anyone else. The District Official immediately took the line that the firm could not interfere with the appointment of an official and they would have to accept Bill Johnson's appointment without question. The firm were informed of the appointments and it was not for them to dictate whether a person was fit for office or not. If the person had been nominated by the group, they obviously were happy to have him as their representative, and if the branch had duly appointed him in accordance with their rules, then the firm could not object or refuse to recognise anyone. The three union officials decided that there would need to be a meeting with management immediately.

A meeting was convened between the three union officials and the Production Manager and Director and the Personnel Officer the next day. The meeting was a formal affair, where the union registered an official complaint and stated that if the firm did not recognise Bill Johnson as a union official immediately then there would be an official dispute. Not wishing to pre-empt a branch decision, the union side said that it was almost certain there would be an immediate stoppage of work. Management stated that they were unhappy with the appointment of Bill Johnson on the grounds that customarily nominees had been with the firm for a reasonable length of time and that two months was far too short. They hinted that they suspected the appointment did not comply with the union's rules. This merely elicited a stern rebuke from the District Official not to meddle in the union's internal affairs. The Personnel Manager tried to ascertain the facts regarding the length of Bill Johnson's membership with the General Workers' Union. This only served to antagonise the union officials. The meeting ended with management stating they would consider their position but were not prepared to give any undertaking on recognising Bill Johnson as shop steward.

Intelligence gathering

The foreman from Bill Johnson's department was having a quiet pint in his local pub when he remembered that one of the members of the pub's dart team worked for a firm that Bill Johnson had previously worked for. He went over to the man and entered into conversation with him. He skilfully turned the conversation round to unions and casually enquired which union organised the shop floor at their firm. He was surprised to hear that it was the Plastics Industry Workers' Union. He then made a mental note of this interesting fact. The foreman passed on the intelligence he had gathered the previous night to the Production Manager who in turn passed it on to the Personnel Officer and the Production Director.

The culminating act

The union, for their part, had called an urgent branch committee meeting. All the newly appointed officials were called, including Bill Johnson. While the District Official knew that the subject would be a delicate one to handle, he decided to go ahead with the meeting. The meeting decided that they would be solidly behind the decision to insist on the acceptance of Bill Johnson as a union official, although one or two did not see eye to eye with Bill. They did not pass a motion to call a full branch meeting nor to recommend industrial action at that stage. The District Official opposed any action that was rushed and ill-considered. When pressed he declined to state specific reasons and the meeting gained the impression that he knew more than he was prepared to make public. After the meeting he took the branch secretary on one side and admitted that Bill Johnson did not fulfil the union's requirements on length of membership. When Bill Johnson had joined Kingston Plastics he had put in an application for union membership directly to the district office. He had asked that his previous period of membership with the Plastics Industry Workers' Union be added to his membership of the General Workers' Union. Although a strange request, the District Official had agreed to it as Bill had offered to pay back-dated subscriptions.

After the branch committee meeting had disbanded, Bill Johnson returned to work. Later that shift Bill was approached by another worker with a complaint about the safety device on his machine which was not working properly. Always keen to take up problems, Bill went to see the shift foreman. The foreman asked why Bill was taking up the matter. Bill said he was the shop steward and was entitled to take up complaints. The foreman replied that to his knowledge Bill was not a shop steward and he was to return to work. Bill replied that he was the duly elected union official and if the foreman insisted in refusing to recognise his position he would report that to his members. Bill left the foreman's office and was seen talking animatedly to several of the department's operators. The foreman contacted the Production Manager immediately and told him of the position.

Exercises

1 As Production Manager, what would you do in the immediate situation?

2 The branch secretary is informed of the incident. He arrives on the scene as Bill is still talking to the operators. As branch secretary what advice would you give your members?

3 List the possible outcomes that might arise from this incident. Which do you think to be the most likely? Describe the factors that will influence the possible outcomes.

4 Role play a meeting convened between the Production Director, Production Manager, Personnel Officer, District Official, branch secretary and branch chairperson. Negotiate to resolve the dispute. Prior to the meeting both sides should prepare notes on how they are going to approach the negotiations, the points they wish to secure and the ones they are prepared to discuss.

5 As an industrial relations consultant engaged by the firm, what detailed changes would you recommend that the firm make to their industrial relations and associated personnel policies to rectify the situation. Also what steps should be taken to restore normal relations between the firm and the union?

6   As the District Official, prepare a report on the incident to your Regional office. State what you believe to be the causes of the dispute and what action should be taken by the union to prevent problems like this happening again.

7   The Managing Director, on his return from a sales trip abroad several days after the events above, has been briefed on the situation. He has recommended that Bill be dismissed for dishonesty (the false statements made on his application form) and that should pre-empt any further discussion on the matter of Bill being a shop steward. The dismissal is to be non-negotiable and Bill should be summarily dismissed immediately.

   As Production Director, prepare a paper for the Managing Director on your reactions to this instruction.

Case 17
The shop floor worker

Analysis

Since the Sex Discrimination Act 1975 and the Equal Pay Act 1970 came into force employers have been forced to pay attention to the differentials that often exist in workplaces between the jobs men and women perform and the pay they receive. The application of the detailed requirements of the Equal Pay Act in workplaces has raised a number of difficult problems. Very often there are differences of interpretation and the lack of explicit job definitions, for example in the form of job descriptions, makes the situation even more difficult. Sometimes job titles are different but the jobs are, except for minor details, the same and any pay differentials are discriminatory. In other instances men and women are ostensibly performing the same job, with the same title, but men receive a higher rate of pay because they perform some tasks that the women do not. This case illustrates a problem of this kind where there is equality but not entirely!

Background knowledge

In this case you are required to examine a situation and highlight the inequalities that exist in a firm. Some may be deliberate, others purely innocent.

Before starting this case you should have some prior knowledge of:

1 organisational structures, hierarchies and promotions policies;
2 personnel and remuneration policies;
3 equal opportunities practices and policies;
4 the law, and its interpretation, on equal opportunities and especially equal pay (Equal Pay Act 1970);
5 the Code of Practice, Equal Opportunities Policies, Procedures and Practices in Employment (issued by the Equal Opportunities Commission).

The company

The Waterhead Mouldings Company was established in a small rural location 22 years ago. It has a workforce of 150, many of whom live locally. This has led to a stable workforce with exception of the younger women who tend to leave school and work for the firm for a few years until they marry and have a family. Even then they often return after a period of time and the firm considers applications from ex-employees favourably. The firm does not pay highly but for the area gives average pay and alternative employment is difficult to find. The firm is rather paternalistic but the atmosphere within it is very friendly, with many people knowing each other or being related.

The firm makes moulds and moulding machinery for the plastics and rubber moulding industry. There is a manufacturing department, which employs skilled tool makers. Supporting this is a stores area which houses all the raw materials including the steel, fasteners, fabrications, seals and so on. The stores personnel, of whom there are ten, are unskilled. They act as the goods inwards department, the stores issue to production and a store for part-finished goods and various pieces of production equipment. Most of the administration is performed by two clerks in the stores. There is a great deal of flexibility amongst the staff with the stores personnel performing most of the jobs as and when required and this suits everyone. However, as is the case in other parts of the firm, jobs have evolved piecemeal to suit the circumstances of the time rather than according to any plan.

Unionisation

The firm is unionised with the toolmakers in a craft union and the rest of the firm, including the stores area, in a general union. There have been few disagreements which have upset the settled atmosphere at Waterhead Moulding and the union officials have rarely had much to do. Usually any matters arising are dealt with in an unofficial and friendly way. This is true for the stores area as well. One of the stores personnel is the shop steward but the job is something of a sinecure. Where changes are made the manager informs the steward. There are also annual pay negotiations to deal with. Apart from this there is little call on the steward to do very much.

Equal opportunities investigated

About two years ago the union's regional office sent out some literature on the workings of the Sex Discrimination Act and the Equal Pay Act and said they were instigating a drive to enforce the letter and the intent of the law. Waterhead Mouldings was targeted by the union as one place where there might be some work to be done to bring the firm's practices into line. The unofficial senior steward went to see Jim Bolton, the Personnel Officer to raise the issue of equality. After some discussion the two agreed that a small committee should be set up to investigate this area of the firm's operations. Both agreed that neither knew much about the subject or how well the firm was implementing the law. They also agreed that the committee would have to include some women. Subsequently the committee was formally constituted. It included the personnel officer, as chairman, a female representative from the office (albeit not a union official, as the office union representative was currently a man), a female representative from the production department (again not the official union representative) and the office manager. It was agreed that in the event of a tie the committee would vote for a change in favour of female members of staff.

The committee met quite frequently initially, then less often as they seemed to lose momentum. They found a number of instances of discrimination in the firm and also it was noted that the senior positions in the firm were all occupied by men. For the latter it was decided to positively assist women in the junior positions to take training courses and for them to be given the opportunity to perform jobs that would enhance their potential for promotion. In the manufacturing department this solution could not work as all the operatives were men. The firm said they would consider employing women in such positions but there had never been any applications from women for such jobs. Ironically it was the unions who were held to blame for the male domination of the toolmaking trade with their recruitment policies for apprenticeships.

The stores area

It was in the stores that there were found to be considerable problems. There were three grades of storeperson (except that all the documentation referred to them as storemen). These were:

(a) Senior storeman – a position of section leader/leading hand, where the person would be responsible for all the work in the stores. Currently there is a man in this position and he arrived at the position based on the usual internal rule of seniority. He is responsible for incoming stores and internal stores.

(b) Storeman – a senior grade in the stores covering all the tasks in the stores. This would typically include accepting delivery notes, checking documentation, arranging off-loading, signing notes, assigning locations for stock and issuing stock. There is currently a man and a woman in this position. Again this position is achieved by seniority from the lowest grade in the stores.

(c) Picker/packer – a position where the person handles stores and stock from locations within the stores area to the production department and helps off-load incoming goods and puts them in their correct location. They have to check that the documentation is correct for part numbers, locations, quantities and for putting the documents out to the correct departments. There are five people in this position; all but one are women.

The committee was concerned that this area in particular needed to be investigated thoroughly as there were a number of discriminatory situations. A further complication that came to light, after enquiries into pay rates, was that the male storemen had a slightly higher rate of pay than the women. This had arisen historically as the result of a claim that men had to do all the lifting work and had to climb up steep ladders onto a mezzanine floor that the women would not go up to. The differential amounted to 2.2p per hour.

Exercises

Stage 1

1 Role play the committee as it investigates the situation in the firm and in particular the stores. The remit for the committee is 'to investigate the situation and to make recommendations to achieve equality of opportunity for all employees, with special reference to the stores area'.

2 Prior to the investigation prepare a file of notes on the case and collect material for:
   (a) the personnel manager, and
   (b) the trade union officials.

3 As an independent observer/consultant give your advice to the firm on what they need to do to bring practices into line with the law and the Code of Practice issued by the Equal Opportunities Commission.
   Include specific recommendations on a system that the firm could set up to monitor equal opportunities within the firm, the way the situation should be reviewed and the measures that need to be taken to rectify areas of discrimination.

4 As for **3**, but acting for the union.

5 Prepare a report emanating from the committee of investigation, with emphasis on practical recommendations.

Stage 2

The outcome of the investigation is that all the stores personnel are to be treated equally, the pay differentials are to be ended and the rules on promotion are to be amended.
   A few days after the publication of the report there was an incident in the

stores. The one woman on the middle grade was performing her duties as normal when the senior storeperson requested that she go onto the mezzanine floor to carry out a stock check. She immediately refused, saying that she was not going up the ladder and walking round the narrow flooring. The other man on the same grade heard of this and also refused to carry out the job on the grounds that every one was equal and that included doing an identical job. The senior storeperson reported this to the production manager.

1 As the Production Manager, what action would you take? List the factors to take into account, the principles you would employ and make a plan of action. Who would you consult? What would you do immediately and in the near future?

2 As the stores shop steward, what advice would you give to the woman in the incident? As the men are also in the union, how will this affect the situation? The production manager is taking this as a refusal to obey a legitimate instruction and as such it is serious. Under the disciplinary procedure, it could lead to suspension.

3 The personnel officer has been informed of the incident. Prepare a memo from him giving advice to the production manager on what he ought to do.

4 Convene a special meeting of the equal opportunities sub-committee to examine this latest incident. Make recommendations to solve the problem.

5 The matter later becomes a matter of dispute. Convene a disputes committee and negotiate a settlement. Include the production manager, the personnel manager, the shop steward, a district union official and a member of the employers' association on the committee.

Case 18

The competent drunk

Analysis

When dealing with matters of discipline one of the important principles to be applied is the need to be seen to be fair and consistent. This is one of the arguments for having a disciplinary procedure. If people are treated fairly and consistently then there is often little ground for complaint. It is notable that frequently in the tribunal cases that lead to an award for unfair dismissal, the case is won or lost because the employer did not treat the employee fairly or as prescribed by a procedure not because the employer had no grounds for dismissal. The case which follows illustrates this.

Background knowledge

When disciplining employees there is always a need to be seen to be fair and consistent. We all have an acute sense of justice and justice must be seen to be done. Procedures can help this process as they should be applied to everyone in the same manner. This is not to suggest that some discretion should not be applied. A good procedure should allow for this. The rigid application of firm rules can be seen as injust as the opposite. The behaviour of supervisors and managers towards their colleagues must be consistent with that shown towards subordinates otherwise there is a cry of 'a law for them and a law for us'.

Before starting this case you should have some prior knowledge of:

1   the principles and practice of discipline and disciplinary action;
2   the role of the supervisor and manager in applying standards of behaviour at work;
3   the problems caused by an inconsistent approach to handling discipline.

Introduction

The PrintaPosta Co is a small printing firm specialising in printing posters. Its work is varied and the firm has built up a reputation, in the face of fierce competition, for its artwork and ability to produce high quality colour work. The firm employs 28 people in the design, production and despatch departments. The atmosphere is friendly but it often gives the impression of frenzied activity as the firm endeavours to achieve delivery dates. On occasions it takes on too much work but would rather over-stretch itself than lose orders.

The competent drunk

The production section employs 15 people and is headed by a print worker of 24 years experience. Jack Hall knows his trade well but has found life more than a little difficult in recent years because of the changes in technology. Jack has been with the firm since it began 15 years ago and the firm is very loyal to him for his hard work and dedication. Jack helped the firm through the first, difficult years and often he put in many more hours than he was paid for, just to see the work completed. The founder of the firm is aware of Jack's shortcomings but relies on him to run the production side of the enterprise while he concentrates on the design side. Jack is a good manager and can get the best out of people.

As a result of the added complexity of printing work and the need to keep up with the technological developments in the field, PrintaPosta created the post of Technical Supervisor last year. They recruited Phil Coggins a young, recently qualified print technician to take on the technical side of the production section's work. This left Jack to concentrate on managing the department. Phil settled into the job relatively quickly and proved to be very good at his job. The firm is happy with the appointment and many of the technical problems that the firm had have now been solved.

However, there is one grave difficulty that has arisen. Phil has a drink problem. He has taken to going out at lunch times to meet his drinking partner and often comes back incapable of doing much work. On many occasions Jack has had to take Phil home in his car to ensure that Phil does not cause a disturbance or get into any danger. This has been noticed by the operatives in the section but the matter has not been brought to the attention to anyone else. Jack feels rather protective of Phil because he relies on him so much for the technical support he provides. If anything, Jack has covered up for Phil and tries to be very discrete in dealing with a situation he finds rather embarrassing.

Lately the situation has deteriorated so much that Phil has taken to having Monday mornings off quite frequently to recover from his heavy week-end drinking sessions. To cover himself when he returns he certifies himself sick as suffering from something other than a bad hangover. Jack tries to support Phil by making excuses for his absences but finds it more difficult on the occasions he returns to work drunk. Nothing has been said to Jack by any of the production department workers but he detects some unease about the situation and is lost to know what to do. He has spoken to Phil about the situation and Phil recognises that he needs to moderate his drinking but then, after a period of time off, falls back into his bad habits again.

One morning Pam, an operative on one of the new, recently installed machines, comes to see Jack. She tells Jack that she has had a life long friend staying with her from Canada and the friend is due to return to Canada that day. Pam asks if she can finish two hours early that day so that she can go to the airport with her friend. Jack, being under considerable pressure to finish a number of jobs that day, including the one on Pam's machine, says he cannot allow her the time off. He says that he had intended to ask her to work over that night to finish the work. Pam becomes very irate and says 'You can let that lazy, drunken technician of yours have days off to go drinking but not an hour off for someone who never has any time off. We've noticed you taking him home after lunch because he's had too much booze. But you wouldn't take me to the airport in your car. I've had enough of this two-faced lot here'. At which she storms out the office, slamming the door.

Pam returns to her machine but is unable to concentrate on her work. At break time she tells all her colleagues about the incident. They support Pam and say they are prepared to back her. Still feeling incensed she changes and leaves the works without saying anything to Jack. She tells her friends they can tell Jack that she's in the pub waiting to stop Phil having too much to drink at lunch time.

Pam turns up for work the next day.

Exercises

1   What would you do if you were Jack:
   (a) when you found out that Pam had left the works;
   (b) when Pam returned the next day.

2   Give your written recommendations to the owner on what action the firm ought to take with regard to:
   (a) Phil's situation;
   (b) disciplinary action against Phil;
   (c) disciplinary action against Pam;
   (d) Jack's managerial performance.

3   As Jack, on reflection, what should you have done from the outset with regard to Phil? Detail the mistakes that you think you made and how you could have avoided them.

4 As the owner of PrintaPosta, state what systems you would institute to avoid the kinds of problems, highlighted in this case, occurring again. State what principles you would use as a guide for good managerial practice.

5 Role play a meeting between Pam, Jack and the owner called to discuss the incident of Pam leaving.

6 The owner has decided that Jack must deal with Phil and that the two must meet to resolve the situation.
  (a) State the guidelines you would issue to Jack for the meeting.
  (b) As Jack, prepare some notes for the meeting with Phil.
  (c) Role play the meeting between Jack and Phil.

7 Write the documents that arise out of this incident. As Jack has dealt with these, write a letter/memo from Jack to:
  (a) Pam, based on the outcome of Exercise 5;
  (b) Phil, based on the outcome of Exercise 6.

Case 19

The skittles player

Analysis

One of the problems that all managers and supervisors have to face when dealing with discipline is that of whether to apply the rules rigidly, whatever the consequences, or whether to be more flexible. When rules are applied rigidly there is the danger of committing an injustice while if there is some flexibility there can be complaints of unfairness, favouritism or victimisation. Also care needs to be taken in drafting the wording of a rule. A rule that includes the words 'may be' is quite different from one which states 'will be'.

Background knowledge

There is often a tendency to apply the saying 'rules were made to be broken' in order to reduce the harshness of rigidly applying rules. Particularly where the rule is not crucial, supervisors and managers tend to allow some flexibility as part of their human relations management. This can become complex where personalities are involved and any relaxation of the rules may well depend on the relationship that exists between the people involved.

Before starting this case you should have some prior knowledge of:

1 the construction and wording of works rules;
2 the application of rules, the case for and against discretion and flexibility in applying rules;
3 disciplinary action arising from a breach of rules;
4 human relations, individual behaviour and supervisor/subordinate relationships.

Introduction

The Plasmould Co runs a two-shift system: 6.00am until 2.00pm and 2.00pm until 10.00pm. The early and late hours sometimes give some difficulty for supervision as there are no managers around to keep an eye on things; nor are they directly available if there was trouble. The late shift is often more trouble because, frequently, working unsocial hours means that requests are made for time off that supervision clearly cannot accede to. As a result of this the Works Rule Book contains a rule saying that 'No one may leave the factory during working hours unless he/she has the express permission of his/her senior supervisor'. Contravention of this rule is specified in the disciplinary procedure as one which 'leads to disciplinary action but is not an offence leading to summary dismissal'.

The skittles match

Jim Carter has worked for Plasmould Co for six years on alternate morning and afternoon shifts. He is a well-liked member of the shift and has established himself as a future potential supervisor. He is a good machine operator and has shown good organisational ability. The one dark cloud is that he knows the senior foreman outside of work and they do not get on. They have quarrelled and their relationship at work is cool.

One Wednesday evening Jim approached his chargehand, Chris Tomkins, with a request. He asked to be given permission to leave the plant for two hours. He was in the local skittles team and, being one of their best players, did not want to miss a crucial match. Knowing that the company was trying to minimise the amount of time off granted and the pressure that the firm was under, Chris said he would have to ask the senior foreman first because he didn't have the authority to give permission to leave.

Chris went about his work setting up the shift and dealing with the usual round of minor problems. The request from Jim slipped his mind. Later Jim came to him for a reply saying that he really needed to go as the game started in 15 minutes. Chris had not seen the senior foreman and because he was tied up on a rather difficult problem said yes to Jim. Again Chris thought nothing more and carried on dealing with the problem.

A little later, as Chris was sorting out another problem, an operator told Chris that the senior foreman was on his rounds and was heading in their direction. Suddenly Chris remembered that he had forgotten to ask permission for Jim to go to the skittles match. Realising that the situation spelt trouble for both of them he decided to go and find Jim and get him back to work immediately. Before Chris arrived back the senior foreman arrived and enquired where Chris was.

Exercises

1 As senior foreman, what would you do in respect of Chris and Jim, after they've come back to work. Also what would you do in terms of taking future action. Write any internal documentation arising out of this situation. Take into account the outcome of Exercises **2** and **3**.

2 The senior foreman wishes to see Jim first. As Jim, how would you approach this meeting and what will you say?

3 As Chris, you are called to a meeting with the senior foreman. What will you say at this meeting?

4 The matter has been referred to you as Production Manager. State what action you would take against Chris and Jim. Explain what you would take into consideration in arriving at your decision. Specify the detailed procedure you would use in implementing your decision. Describe the possible pitfalls you would try to avoid.

5 Write up any documentation that arises out of exercise **4**.

6 Write a report on the situation. Make any recommendations relating to changes to current policy and practice that you feel are necessary.

7 Role play the meetings in **2** and **3**.

Case 20

Redundancy at Toolcraft

Analysis

One of the consequences of technological change is that often there has to be a reduction in the workforce. The financial justification for the capital investment is that savings must be made on labour costs. While there is some inevitability about the march of technology, the consequences for the individual firm have to be worked out most carefully. When the numbers employed at a firm need to be reduced the means of achieving this needs to be worked out jointly, preferably using some agreed procedure. Where agreement is not secured the outcome may be disasterous. This case takes place in a small firm where these questions are raised but not satisfactorily answered.

Background knowledge

In this case you will be examining a situation where a firm is introducing some new machinery, to improve methods and cut labour costs, and the consequent need to reduce the workforce. Initially this was not planned as a redundancy situation but subsequently became one.

Before starting this case you should have some prior knowledge of:

1 the justification and implications of a shift to capital intensive manufacture;
2 the means of achieving the reduction in human resources required as a result of 1;
3 the skills in handling such a situation;
4 group behaviour and dynamics;
5 the need for, and form of, consultations and communication in a firm;
6 the definition of redundancy and the procedures for handling redundancy.

The firm

Toolcraft is a light engineering firm that produces small components for the car industry on a sub-contract basis. Its strength lies in its craftsmen's skills to produce very high quality work to exacting standards. Although tied to the motor trade it has maintained a reasonably healthy order book overall but with some minor hic-cups from time to time, which reflects the fortunes of the industry. It is a small firm, employing 55 people. Toolcraft is located in the Midlands, and it has a high level of union membership amongst its employees as a result of recruiting people from the engineering industry.

Industrial relations is fair, with an uneasy peace existing between the workers and management. This situation is partially a result of the firm always having to seek new orders to keep going. It rarely gets an order that keeps all the workforce occupied for more than a few weeks. This leads to a rather piece-meal approach to long term planning because of the uncertainty of future orders. Another consequence is that rumours are often rife that the firm is going through a bad patch and that jobs are under threat. Again this is often fuelled by management refusing to talk about issues, due to this uncertainty, and by them often saying that if certain demands are made then that would jeopardise future business. Costs necessarily need to be pared to the bone in order to successfully tender for contracts.

The tool room

The production department is where industrial relations can be the most difficult. The majority of the workforce work in the two main departments and they are virtually closed shops. There have been one or two minor stoppages in recent times but nothing too devastating. The tool room however is not in the same category. Although all the men are highly trained engineers and are considered the elitist group amongst engineering staff, at Toolcraft they have an exemplary record. They are all in the union and have a great deal of loyalty to the union but are independently minded enough to decide for themselves what they will do rather than just follow the shop floor on an issue. Hence they did not follow the shop floor out during a recent stoppage. The tool room has a good record of efficiency and an enviable record on quality. As they are located away from the shop floor they keep themselves to themselves. As a group they are very cohesive and get on well with each other.

The dominant personality within the group is Chris Savage. He was the shop steward until recently and still remains the group's unofficial spokesman. While the group has a shop steward they nearly always defer to Chris for his advice. He is an excellent craftsman and is respected by everyone. The foreman of the tool room is Geoff Bostock who is also a very good craftsman, having served his time in the trade and is still reckoned to be one of the best. He knows his men well and makes certain he keeps in touch. The record within the tool room is largely due to this atmosphere and Geoff often boasts about his enviable record to the other supervisors in the firm. The men, although particularly independently minded, always meet Geoff Bostock's requests and never have much cause to complain.

Due to the fluctuating level of orders, when orders are won they are always needed 'yesterday' and there is quite a lot of overtime worked when delivery dates are tight. This topic alone has caused more problems than any other within the production departments. The amount of overtime and its allocation always causes difficulty and unrest. It is almost impossible to plan it regularly but when it is needed it requires a flexible attitude by everyone. While the problem has been the subject of numerous discussions, there is still no workable solution. In the tool room the situation is different. They have a more flexible approach to moving round on the jobs they are currently working on. The amount of overtime is calculated by Geoff Bostock and then the detail on who comes in is worked out in conjunction with Chris Savage.

New machinery

In recent times the firm have been investigating new methods of manufacture in the tool room. Although the firm is able to produce the very highest quality product they are being beaten by the new methods that some of their competitors are employing. As a result of a number of orders being lost in recent times, the management have decided that the only way to remain in competition is to invest in some new equipment that will keep them in the market. A number of the older machines will have to be replaced and the level of automation on the new machines means that less labour will be required in the tool room. An estimation by management is that one person would have to leave the tool-room. Geoff Bostock has been appraised of this and has had a private word with Chris Savage. The plan is that the last man in be transferred out of the tool room into the maintenance department where there is a requirement for a skilled man. This would mean a loss of earnings. The man selected, Bill Green, has been told about the position by Geoff Bostock.

The news was taken badly by everyone, and particularly by Bill Green. The men thought that the new equipment would need a period of commissioning and that the workload of the department would increase over time anyway. They had accepted Bill into their group and assessed him as a competent craftsman who they did not want to lose. Bill refused the proposed move and made an official complaint to the shop steward. Discussions ensued and these did not get very far as management still considered that there would be a reduced work level in the tool room. They argued that the only economic basis for the investment in new equipment was to reduce labour costs. Both sides gradually got further entrenched in their respective positions and there was no obvious solution. The matter came to head on a Friday, when Bill Green received his redundancy notice. The tool room staff walked out immediately.

Exercises

1 As production manager specify what you will do immediately you are aware of the walk-out. Prepare a brief for the Managing Director on the issues raised and the possible solutions for the immediate situation.

2 A meeting has been called between the production manager, Geoff Bostock, the union District Officer and Chris Savage. Role play the meeting to negotiate a settlement. Prior to the meeting both sides should meet separately to decide their strategy and tactics. Prepare notes specifying the main issues, what you are prepared to negotiate and what is non-negotiable.

3 As a consultant to the firm, write a report suggesting what changes should be made within the firm. Base this on the object lessons of this incident.

4 You are a trainee in the offices and the Managing Director has asked you to help formulate some ideas on the issues raised. Draw up a list of the possible ways in which a firm can reduce its labour force, over time. Evaluate each policy and recommend a preferred range of policies and specify the ones you reject.

5 As a trainer with a local firm you have been asked to do some training for Toolcraft. Prepare some notes for a trainir.g session to be held for all the supervisors and managers at Toolcraft. The topic is 'the management of change'.

6 Geoff Bostock has come to you to ask for some advice. When there is a return to work (make some assumptions about the final outcome) he is worried how to carry on with the proposed programme of technological updating in the tool-room. Advise him of the human relations aspects of how to deal with this problem. Use the report in Exercise 3 to help.

7 Use the Technology Agreement, from Case 6 and apply it to this case. Run Exercise 2 but with both sides applying the procedural Technology Agreement from the point where there is an original proposal to introduce new equipment into the tool room.

Appendix

Learning points

This section is intended to give tutors and students a guide to what should have been learnt from the cases. These are not model answers; in most instances there is no *one* correct answer. It is for the participants to arrive at a justifiable conclusion using the concepts, principles, theories, points of law, etc. they know.

Case 1

One of the central features of collective bargaining and industrial relations is negotiating the terms and conditions of employment. It gives meaning to the representative nature of our collective bargaining system and the importance of negotiations. The case illustrates the way in which pay negotiations are conducted in practice and the various aspects of this. In particular you should have learnt about the following:

1 the exchange of information prior to negotiations, direct and indirect hints and signals;

2 the communication channels that are used to disseminate information such as committees, house newspapers, rumour and others;

3 the posturing by the sides to the negotiations to create a climate that is favourable to their side's claim, such as the claim of lower profits;

4 the role of managers, the trade union officials and committees in formulating strategy and tactics. Prior to any negotiations the sides prepare themselves thoroughly by collecting facts and data, marshalling their arguments, predicting the others side's reaction to proposals and deciding what is negotiable and what is not;

5 the statements of claim and counter-claim that are made to start negotiations, where the sides make their case known. This calls for careful listening skills to detect the signals being sent;

6 the process of bargaining and the use of arguments and trading within negotiations to arrive at a final agreement;

7 the use of sanctions to reinforce a claim. This may be posturing and

bluff or it may be for real. It is one of the means of trying to secure an agreement by showing how strongly a side feels about an issue;
8   the termination of negotiations, the re-assessment of positions and the re-commencement of negotiations. Often difficult negotiations are not concluded in one meeting. After the first meeting the sides can reconsider their position and adjust tactics in the light circumstances.

Case 2

As firms grow from small beginings to larger enterprises the managers of the firm must pay attention to the structures that are necessary in an expanding firm. While firms are small, matters can be dealt with personally and informally. Beyond a certain size of firm, this is no longer possible and there is a need for greater formality (though this does not imply rigidity). There is a need for personnel policies and procedures that ensure fair treatment for all employees. In particular you should have learnt about the following:
1   commercially the firm grew to be successful but little attention was paid to the internal needs of the organisation. Beyond a certain size a firm has to have a structure and there must be a formal means of communication, including matters relating to industrial relations;
2   the communication structure needs to include hearing the voice of the employees on a range of matters. For managers to be unaware of what is really happening in a firm demonstrates how remote people can be from each other;
3   not all employees will readily identify with or have a 100% commitment to a firm without there being some reciprocal benefit to themselves. To expect total commitment, even from the new starters in the business, is not possible without the managers working for this. The motivation displayed by the owners may not always 'rub off'. A pay and rewards structure is needed. Similarly a grading structure is needed to enable employees to perceive and pursue a career path for themselves;
4   while all enterprises have to ensure success if only to survive, there needs to be a blend of the commercial with the human. If firms always see action in terms of efficiency and cost effectiveness without showing under-standing of people's problems then morale will suffer. Employee rights must be safeguarded;
5   outside agencies are fine for giving advice and for consultations but they are no substitute for tackling the problems within the firm. Often the only people who can solve the difficulties are the managers and employees of the firm. Delegating the examination of the firm to a consultant was no real answer;
6   there has to be an accommodation of other people's points of view and open discussion and negotiation can achieve this. Not to reach such an accommodation leaves the problems unsolved which can lead to future unrest.

Case 3

A fundamental issue in industrial relations is the existence of good, workable agreements. In their absence, or if the agreements or procedures are poor, this is bound to lead to trouble. The case illustrates how problems can mount if discipline is not tackled properly. In particular you should have learnt about the following:

1   the need for a well thought out, coordinated policy towards discipline so all the managers (including supervisors) in a firm know and operate the same procedure consistently. Inconsistency leads to chaos and dispute;

2   the negotiation of an agreed disciplinary procedure, so that employees are committed to the procedure working as well as management;

3   the construction of a disciplinary procedure, incorporating the points of the official Code of Practice on disciplinary action. Apart from anything else this will reduce the chance of successful claims for unfair dismissal;

4   the consistent and fair application of that procedure so that justice is being seen to be done;

5   how to deal with difficult cases sensitively such as the case of the older employee who has been late and the suspected criminal;

6   the need for support by senior managers so that junior managers and supervisors know that when they do take action that they will be supported in what they do.

Case 4

Dealing with redundancies is always difficult. There is no easy way but there are better ways than making a mere written declaration that so many will go. In this case you should have explored the possibilities for minimising the impact of the need to reduce manpower and the need for clear procedures on consultation and handling redundancies. In particular you should have learnt about the following:

1   the mistakes that the firm made in the first incident of redundancies. Clearly just posting a notice is not treating people with respect and is likely to cause ill-feeling at least, if not precipitate a dispute. There should be a period of consultation during which various possibilities can be explored, such as early retirement and voluntary redundancies;

2   the legal requirements for consultations and handling redundancies might not apply here, being a firm without a recognised trade union. However, this does not prevent the spirit of the law applying as a matter of good practice;

3   using a 'last in, first out' redundancy policy may be the way to minimise redundancy payments but the implications in terms of manpower planning and the personal impact of redundancy can make it a poor policy;

4   the need for sensitivity in dealing with a situation that affects the lives of other people. The impact of redundancy can be minimised and arguably firms should develop policies and procedures to do so.

Case 5

Arbitration is an important last stage in a procedure as any failure of arbitration leaves no other means of negotiating an end to the dispute except by a war of attrition or 'sitting it out.' There are a number of variations on the theme of arbitration and this case aims to allow students to examine the detail of the clauses making up an arbitration agreement (or a stage within another procedure). In particular you should have learnt about the following:

1 the function of arbitration in resolving a dispute by the sides to the dispute presenting their case and the arbitrator making an independent decision;

2 the role and function of the various actors in arbitration such as unions, management and arbitrator plus advisors and representatives;

3 the place of arbitration in a procedure as a last stage when the normal agreements have yeilded a final failure to agree;

4 the points to be considered on the appointment of an arbitrator, the statements of claim, the exchange of statements, time limits, the arbitration hearing, whether the findings are binding or not and the publication of the findings. Many of these are matters of opinion and practice does vary. You should have analysed the strengths and weaknesses of the various arguments on these issues;

5 the relative merits of pendulum arbitration and its possible use, particularly in making both sides to a dispute moderate their claims.

Case 6

At the heart of the collective bargaining structure is the process of negotiating. It is the means by which agreement is reached between employers and employees. There are considerable skills attached to negotiating and as with all skills they can only be improved through practice. This case (and the next two) aim to provide realistic scenarios in which students can acquire and practice these skills. In particular you should have learnt about the following:

1 the need for careful preparation before negotiations commence. This will involve marshalling your arguments, collecting facts and data, deciding what points you are prepared to concede and stick on and predicting the other side's arguments and counter arguments;

2 the skills of presenting a case and listening to the other side's case, plus bargaining, trading, conceding, sending signals and closing, plus agreeing on the form of words of the final agreement;

3 the use of procedural agreements for use as the framework within which action is taken on an issue, i.e. in this case where changes are taking place as a result of technological change;

4 the impact of technology on the number of jobs and the type of job within organisations. The need to minimise the fear of job loss and job skills;

5 to provide a means for employees to be consulted and to be kept informed about change;

6 the need to assess training/re-training needs in the process of change.

7 assessing the health and safety implications of the technology being introduced (though not to include technical details in a procedural agreement).

Case 7

At the heart of the collective bargaining structure is the process of negotiating. It is the means by which agreement is reached between employers and employees. There are considerable skills attached to negotiating and as with all skills they can only be improved through practice. This case provides you with the opportunity to test these skills on what is not an easy topic, i.e. the closed shop. The main problem is remaining objective and not allowing personal views and prejudices preventing a discussion with a view to reaching an agreement. In particular you should have learnt about the following:

1 the need for careful preparation before negotiations commence. This will involve marshalling your arguments, collecting facts and data, deciding what points you are prepared to concede and stick on and predicting the other side's arguments and counter arguments;

2 the skills of presenting a case and listening to the other side's case plus bargaining, trading, conceding, sending signals and closing, as well as agreeing on the form of words of the final agreement;

3 the use of procedural agreements for use as the framework within which action is taken on an issue. Where a closed shop is being contemplated this agreement can be used or, (more likely) where certain points arise during the operation of a closed shop, the agreement should provide the framework within which an answer could be found;

4 the complexity of the law relating to a person who is dismissed from a closed shop for non-membership of a union. The need to comply with the law or run the risk of a civil claim for unfair dismissal (including the union being jointly sued);

5 the balance of power in organisations as between employer and employee. The right, or otherwise, of trade unions, as representative of the employees, to become involved in the decision making processes of an organisation (e.g. recruitment) or to have the power of veto over management's actions (e.g. sub-contractors);

6 the use of ballots in the workplace to test the acceptability or support for certain proposals and the legal standards set for support of a closed shop;

7 the need to deal carefully and sensitively with employees who do not wish to be bound by certain constraints e.g. those who object to joining a trade union.

Case 8

The one procedure that is put to test more often than any other, is the disciplinary procedure. A negotiations procedure may only be used once or twice a year but a disciplinary procedure may well be used every week in larger organisations. This case illustrates the issues that are raised in negotiating such a procedure. Also involved in this case is the process of negotiating. It is the means by which agreement is reached between employers and employees. There are considerable skills attached to negotiating and as with all skills they can only be improved through practice. This case provides you with the opportunity to practice and improve these skills. In particular you should have learnt about the following:

1 the need for careful preparation before negotiations commence. This will involve marshalling your arguments, collecting facts and data, deciding what points you are prepared to concede and stick on and predicting the other side's arguments and counter arguments;

2 the skills of presenting a case and listening to the other side's case plus bargaining, trading, conceding, sending signals and closing, plus agreeing on the form of words of the final agreement;

3 the use of procedural agreements for use as the framework within which action is taken on an issue. Disciplinary action is usually taken in stages and these must be clearly mapped out. The employee must know what these are;

4 the procedure should include the employee's right to be accompanied, to have their side of the case heard and the right to an appeal to another person in the organisation;

5 the need to have the warnings recorded in writing;

6 the use of a variety of sanctions depending on the nature of the offence;

7 to state for which offences an employee can be summarily dismissed;

8 the careful wording of the clauses, especially any rules. The words to look for are 'will', 'might', 'should', 'can' etc..

Case 9

The establishment of even a very basic form of industrial relations in some organisations is difficult. In the hotel industry this difficulty is caused by the transient work force, the dominance of part-time work and the lack of employee organisation. However, this should not prevent the development of policies which provide for greater employee satisfaction in the terms and conditions of employment and how these are determined. This would benefit both employer and employee. This case demonstrates a situation where Mid-Anglia is being forced to address itself to these questions. In particular you should have learnt about the following:

1   the reasons why personnel policies are important to both employer and employee. It is well established that dissatisfied employees do not work as well as satisfied employees. One cause of dissatisfaction is the sense of not knowing or not being involved in the organisation to the extent that the terms and conditions of employment are not subject to joint discussion;

2   the role of the law to set statutory minimum wages and other conditions in industries where industrial relations has not developed, the terms that are laid down and the way in which these are implemented at local level;

3   the arguments for and against trade union recognition, the reasons why employees feel the need for trade union representation and how a claim for recognition can be handled;

4   the role of a conciliator in helping two sides to resolve their differences and come to a joint agreement. This should include the skills of presenting a case orally and in writing and reaching a compromise on contentious issues.

Case 10

One of the trends in the economy during the 1980's has been the growth of industrial holding groups and the move towards fewer companies owning a greater proportion of the economy. Often these holding companies look out for other companies ripe for takeover. Northern Electromotors could well be one of them. It has a marketable product but is inefficient and needs an injection of new ideas and momentum from the top. The case looks at the industrial relations aspects of this. In particular you should have learnt about the following:

1   the formal structure and organisation which is moribund and ineffective. There is no leadership and there are no policies. The informal structure has become important and is very effective e.g. the relationship between the supervisors and the union officials;

2   informal practices have been allowed to become established. These are then very hard to break e.g. allocation of overtime. There is a need to re-establish formal working practices and to ensure these are adhered to, with no unofficial deviation;

3   the benefits of fewer trade unions in an organisation – smoother collective bargaining, less potential for inter-union disputes, a uniform set of terms and conditions of employment etc. e.g. the number of conflicts arising from the two shop floor unions and the supervisors, the position of the staff association and the second staff union;

4   a new management is unlikely to accept the current situation, especially the informal structure and practices. The way in which the changes will be implemented needs to be planned carefully – a gradual approach, the use of consultations, negotiations or by direct instruction. Some practices may be seen as out-of-date and inefficient e.g. individual bonus schemes, promotion by seniority, apprenticeship system, demarcation of craftsmen's jobs and the inflexibility of labour;

5 the lack of clear policies and direction from management has led, in part, to the current situation. Managers seen to acquiesce with a situation are likely to lose any respect when they do try to impose their will. There is a need for clear policies and for them to be implemented to gain the full backing of the workforce.

Case 11

The actions of managers are of fundamental importance in determining whether industrial relations within an enterprise are good or not. Whilst there is no one perfect method, there are certain ground rules that should be observed and taken as good practice. In this case the management of changes in working practices should have included more open communication and cosultation and less of the under-handed, secrecy that did take place. People who are left in the dark fear what they do not know about and are most unlikely to co-operate in any changes unilaterally imposed on them. This will inevitably lead to confrontation and then to a loss of confidence and trust. Retrieving the situation is then an up-hill struggle to achieve mutual trust and respect. In particular you should have learnt about the following:

1 the need to communicate effectively with employees and to provide some means of consultation. Not to even inform the supervisors, let alone involve them in the process of change, was a major error;

2 where distrust exists this will lead to confrontation and resistance to change. The exercise became negative and a battle because people feared what was going on. The final incident that led to the dispute was only a symptom of the trouble not the cause;

3 in cases where large scale changes are aimed for, the processes of collective bargaining should be utilised. To ignore the procedures that have been agreed to be used will again lead to problems;

4 the lack of good management practice is also revealed in the recruitment policy. Perhaps the firm got its due desserts when it employed someone like Stan!

5 the Works Manager clearly wielded too much power and was very autocratic in his use of power. He should have involved the production manager and the supervisors much more and allowed them to perform the day to day activities on the plant under his overall supervision;

6 resolving a dispute of this magnitude is difficult. Relationships are strained and negotiating a settlement will take up much valuable time and energy that could have been expended on more productive tasks. The restoration of normality or improving the situation will take a long time. The union will doubtless try to extract as much as possible in concessions to resolve the dispute;

7 the involvement of a conciliation officer to attempt to achieve a settlement of a claim for unfair dismissal before the case is referred to an industrial tribunal. This may help resolve some of the issues when a neutral, third party investigates a situation and attempts to bring the two sides together;

8 the development of personnel and industrial relations policies that will be used by both management and union to further the prosperity of the firm and its employees. The lack of policies partially contributed to the firm's current problems and formulating and implementing policies may help bring the firm out of its troubles.

Case 12

Whilst management should always retain the right to manage, it is the manner in which managers manage that is of importance in maintaining good industrial relations. This always becomes a matter for extreme care when a new manager is charged with introducing changes in a firm that has some established traditions. The objectives can be achieved but this will only occur with the help and co-operation of all concerned. Trying to push changes through regardless will antagonise and ultimately lead to a challenge and battle of wills. This case illustrates the need to consult and reach agreement rather than dictate. A manager will succeed in achieving better results if the workforce is carried along with the changes instead of being antagonised. The tea-break is probably just the excuse for a show down and is symptomatic of the resentment caused by the insensitive approach made by Roberts. In particular you should have learnt about the following:

1 the need to maintain agreements in working order. Where they are allowed to become changed by 'custom and practice' then altering them later will be difficult;

2 any changes should be made by negotiation and not by stealth. Both sides 'tried it on' and this only led to bad relations developing;

3 where resistance to ideas/proposals is met then the situations needs careful handling. The aggressive approach will be opposed and lead to a war of attrition. Eventually Roberts may need to stand his ground but this should not have occurred immediately on the issue of the tea break. A more subtle approach would possibly have avoided a damaging confrontation;

4 complaints may be justified e.g. on the level of service at break time and should be investigated not dismissed;

5 more innovative solutions could have been suggested or tried. Flexible break times could have overcome some of the problems of queuing or the provision of a vending machine;

6 Roberts seemed not to have anyone in his confidence. He needed to work through his supervisors more to achieve his results. It looks like a one man campaign;

7 communicating sensitive subjects by way of a memo on a notice board was a poor means of communicating with the workforce. It would appear as a threat or challenge, which the men rose to;

8 the difficulty in the future will be restoring normal relations. The meetings to resolve the problem will be tense, with neither side likely to give much.

Case 13

Normally a firm decides how it will act and although it is influenced by external, environmental factors it is rarely dictated by them (expect the law). In this case a situation has developed where the outside organisation (the insurance company) dictates its terms to the company. There could well be a case that the firm should not have allowed Bill Watson to continue in his job when it was apparent that he was unable to cope and it required the insurance company to press this point home. The case provides the scenario for a situation that needs handling with great care and sensitivity. In particular you should have learnt about the following:

1 the need to take positive action promptly when problems arise. To leave them unattended usually leads to further, more serious problems in the future. When it became apparent that Bill's driving record was deteriorating action should have been taken;

2 the action that could have been taken might have included further training, transfer to shorter distance driving, transfer to other non-driving duties. Bill was not made aware of the seriousness of the situation. It appears that the firm became complacent about the situation;

3 there should have been adequate monitors within the firm to highlight the problem and to bring such exceptional behaviour to the attention of senior management. The firm could then have instituted action earlier, perhaps even officially warning Bill about his future conduct;

4 the firm should have faced up to the unpleasant truth of the situation and not have tried to minimise its responsibilities in the matter. They are Bill's employer and have the responsibility to take action. The attempted deal to 'pay Bill off' was wrong and unlawful. You cannot have an agreement for legal action not to be taken, even if the employee agrees initially;

5 Bill can still pursue a claim for unfair dismissal although it is doubtful that he would win. The firm were given little option in the circumstances although their handling of the dismissal was poor. A tribunal could award Bill damages for the poor handling of the situation and the attempted pay-off;

6 assessed against the Code of Practice's recommendations on handling discipline the firm comes out badly. Bill was given no right to be represented, he was offered no appeal and he was merely confronted with the accusations and the outcome (dismissal).

Case 14

Management have a responsibility to get the best out of their employees. They must do what they can to improve the performance of an employee that has been recognised as not doing as well as the organisation requires. This should include help, encouragement and training and the situation should have been monitored to check on the effectiveness of the action taken. The employee should have been involved and made aware of the position. Ultimately, if the employee fails to respond to management's best efforts then disciplinary action can be taken. Any action should be taken with a view to effecting improvement not merely as a negative action that leads ultimately to dismissal. These principles of good managerial practice are all the more important when the employee is a member of management. The case focuses on human relations and managerial action (or inaction). In particular you should have learnt about the following:

1 identifying poor performance. Ms King may well have had her problems but these should have been recognised and dealt with by the senior managers of Auto Silencer. For Alan Carter to bring up such a matter at a meeting was the wrong topic, at the wrong time, in the wrong place. He should have established the exact nature of the problem, had a private word with Ms King and specified what the complaints were against her and helped her to rectify these shortcomings;

2 that having become aware of the problem the firm should have monitored the situation and kept Ms King appraised of her progress or otherwise. She did not get very much in the way of support, certainly not in a practical way, and she was not made aware of how well she was doing. In fact she obviously wished to know how she was doing and was unable to gain access to the senior managers;

3 this lack of support for her in a managerial position is probably just cause to sustain a claim for constructive dismissal. Her actions at work were certainly not justified but the senior managers did nothing to help the situation. You should have recognised this as a case of constructive dismissal not unfair dismissal. The employee gave notice as a result of the employer's actions where it was not possible for her to continue in employment.

Case 15

This case is complex in that it contains three elements i.e. the claim for a closed shop, the refusal of the Asian community to join the union and the incident of violence. In practice it is often the case that several issues are all inter-related and the skill of both union and management is to know how to resolve the separate problems rather than all of them together. The incident of violence can and should be tackled as a separate issue but should be taken as a clear indicator of the poor relations that exist between the two groups (or some sections within the groups). The other two issues are associated and solving one should help solve the other. This will take some skill and tact on the part of the negotiators. In particular you should have learnt about the following:

1 the issues raised by a claim for a closed shop and the principles that various parties are likely to raise as important. Management should be concerned with the overall situation and especially their responsibility to maintaining harmonious relations with the whole of the workforce. Clearly the union is wishing to increase union membership and has chosen the closed shop as a means of doing this. The possibility exists that the aim of 100% membership could be achieved some other way;

2 a closed shop agreement (or union membership agreement) would most probably have to contain clauses that guaranteed the rights of the minority not to join a union, especially where these beliefs are so strongly held by a racial group. They may be a case of indirect discrimination if the union insisted on everyone joining the union. If the management were a party to such an agreement, then the company could also be accused of this;

3 where tension runs high the possibility exists for that tension to boil over into violence. The prank did nothing except cause the rift between the two groups to widen, and was probably designed to do that. Management should monitor the situation closely and ensure that harmonious relations exist and discipline any acts of discrimination. However, the act of violence cannot be condoned and the two will have to be disciplined. This will call for a firm, quick decision to defuse the situation and to show that behaviour of that kind will not be tolerated;

4 race relations in an organisation can be managed and the Code of Practice gives some clear guidance on this, for both management and unions. Many of the points in the Code are relevant to this case. The firm probably needs to monitor the situation more closely and to positively develop its policies in this area.

Case 16

The right of representation is fundamental to collective bargaining as is the right of the union to be independent and free from interference from the employer. This has been recognised at law and unions can now register as independent (of the employer) and indeed some trade union rights are only afforded to independent trade unions. The role of the shop steward is crucial in local level industrial relations and hence the independence of action in appointing union officials is jealously guarded by unions. Any interference is likely to lead to a clear call for 'hands off'. However, there may be cases when management may have grounds for not accepting the will of the union membership to be represented by a person of their choice. To refuse to accept the duly elected person will obviously be seen as an interference, by management, in the independent processes of the union. The grounds for the refusal to accept Bill as shop steward are stated in detail but whether they are justified is for you to decide! In particular you should have learnt about the following:

1 the means of electing a shop steward, the role of the union branch and its members. A frequent problem is that there are few people who wish to stand and unopposed candidates are quite common and there are instances when there are no candidates at all. The latter situation is difficult for management, as to have no union representative for a group can make industrial relations difficult as procedures always assume that there is a representative;

2 the skills needed to handle such a delicate situation. Managers that refuse to recognise a union official need to be sure of the grounds for the refusal as they will be challenged by the union in no uncertain manner. The negotiations to resolve the dispute will be difficult as the union is bound to stand firm on the principle of non-interference by management in its affairs;

3 the recruitment policies and practices were defective. Although there is often pressure to recruit quickly to overcome immediate staff shortage problems, more care in selection might have avoided the problem altogether. The lack of checking Bill's previous employment record and not taking up references was poor practice;

4 whilst the firm issued credentials to newly appointed union officials, the procedure did not specifically allow for a 'reference back' or a challenge to the nominated persons;

5 when the Production Director had taken the decision not to accept Bill, he should have called in the union's senior official or the District Officer to tell them of the decision, not merely excluded Bill's name from a list;

6 dismissing Bill may be a possible solution for the firm but in the short term the firm may have a serious dispute on its hands. If the union affirms the appointment of Bill as a shop steward, dismissing someone the union recognises as an official would be serious. There may well be sufficient grounds to dismiss Bill, e.g. false information on the application form, but dismissal could be a high risk strategy.

Case 17

One of the important employment right's issues that has been campaigned for over the last decade or more has been that of equal opportunities at work. There has been legislation passed, an independent body set up to promote this and more recently a Code of Practice issued. There have been blatant cases of outright discrimination but in the bulk of cases the discrimination has often been indirect and unintentional. Often the custom and practice that exists in a firm tends to make for a situation in which women are treated less favourably than men. This case shows that the rules on promotion, for example, are discriminatory without being designed to be so. In particular you should have learnt about the following:

1 the need to examine job grading schemes, the structure of the work-force, promotion rules, recruitment and selection procedures, training policies and manpower planning to ascertain that they are not discriminatory;

2 in some instances policies that have been used for many years may have yielded a bias within the structure of the workforce. For example a promotions policy based on seniority (a common place policy) can discrimi-nate against young women who have a break in their service to have a family;

3 the law allows certain steps to be taken to alleviate the problems caused over the years e.g. by affording training opportunities to certain groups. However, it is illegal to positively discriminate in favour of a group. A recruitment policy which states that the firm will only recruit women into the next vacancies that arise on the shop floor, for example, would be discriminatory against men and not lawful;

4 a job grading scheme can differentiate between men and women where there is a substantial and justifiable reason. However, this should not be used as a means of discrimination. The latter problem that arose, with the refusal of the woman to go up the ladder, would clearly be used by some to demonstrate the need to differentiate between the jobs that men and women do. Whether this justifies paying the men more is a point for discussion;

5 solving the problems raised may take many years to remove discrimi-nation. You cannot suddenly demote men and promote women to redress the imbalance in the structure of the workforce. By agreeing on policies and implementing them the firm has set off on the road to eliminating discrimi-nation in the firm;

6 there is a need for training in this area to make people aware of the law, to give examples of good practice that exist and to start the process of change within the firm's systems. More than most areas, the area of discrimination needs to effect a change of behaviour and secure people's commitment to the ideals of non-discrimination;

7 unions also need to look at their practices to see if they are operating within the letter and intent of the law. The Code of Practice is also relevant to their operations. Some of the craft unions have tended to maintain prac-tices that have led to the male domination of certain trades. Again positive drives to encourage women to train for these trades is lawful.

Case 18

Consistency is the key word in this case. Clearly Jack was leaving himself wide open to criticism by allowing the situation with Phil to develop to the extent it did and then to deal with Pam in such a strict manner. It could be argued that Pam's reason for asking for leave was a weak one and had Jack not been in the situation he was with Phil, then he would have had considerable grounds for refusing Pam's request. However, the workforce were very much aware of the situation and if Jack 'can do it for Phil, he can do it for us'. This weakens Jack's standing with the rest of the workforce, even if they can sympathise with Jack's predicament. There is also the point that Jack's action is seen as condoning Phil's behaviour. Again this lowers Jack's reputation in the eyes of those he is supervising. In particular you should have learnt about the following:

1   the need for the consistent application of rules to everyone, with exceptions in extenuating circumstances. Certainly Phil was not an exception and he should have been brought to task earlier for the kind of behaviour that he indulged in;

2   management should have been aware of the situation. Keeping 'an ear to the ground' is necessary so that situations like this do not develop. Jack may well have kept this all very quiet but this only exasperated the problem;

3   Jack should be reprimanded for his actions. Even though he may have acted from the best of motives, his actions undermined his authority in the workplace;

4   Phil should be disciplined so that the rest of the workforce realise that his behaviour is no longer acceptable. It may not be too harsh to put him on a final warning stating that any future indiscipline will lead to the sack. However, there may be a need for medical help if the drink problem has got out of control;

5   Jack will need to do a lot to recover from the position he now finds himself in. He has lost his reputation and his standing with the workforce will be very low. Any future disciplinary action will need handling very carefully to establish his authority again.

Case 19

Whilst there are always situations where supervisors need to use their discretion, it is doubtful if Chris should have acted as he did in this case. If an employee has a phone call to say there is a dire emergency at home, then the supervisor (if at all sensitive to the needs of his employees) will allow the person to go immediately. A skittles match is hardly in the same category. Both Chris and Jim would have known the rule and should have adhered to it. The Senior foreman should have been asked. Jim presumably knew in advance, as he had made arrangements for his cover. He could have asked the Senior foreman beforehand. Doubtless the Senior foreman thought the whole the situation had been planned by Chris and Jim to undermine his authority, in contravention of the explicit and clear rules of the works. Chris added to his problems, and produced a tacit admission of his guilt, by leaving the works to fetch Jim. In particular you should have learnt about the following:

1   the need for rules. Plasmould had a rule and employees knew what needed to be done to obtain permission to leave the premises. Also the rule is linked to the disciplinary procedure, as it should be. In the event of contravention, then certain action may/will be taken;

2   the wording of a rule is crucial. The rule about leaving the works is clear and unambiguous – the express permission of the senior foreman is required. This could and should leave the senior foreman discretion on what circumstances he will grant permission. Managers have to be trusted to act fairly and justly. If they do not, then the matter will come to a head sooner or later and changes made to ensure a fairer way of dealing with the situation. In dire emergencies the rule may have to be ignored, for example if the senior foreman could not be found;

3   the disciplinary action arising from breaking the rules is also explicitly stated, although not so unambiguously as the rule itself. 'Leads to' implies some degree of flexibility and again this can be left to the manager concerned to exercise discretion where it is thought just to do so;

4   clear action will need to be taken in this case to show that management will act where necessary and also to maintain the senior foreman's authority. Perhaps some degree of leniency could be shown as the two acted quite innocently in the circumstances (although the senior foreman would take some convincing!). If no action is taken about leaving work for a skittles match then the firm would deserve to have a problem of indiscipline on its hands in the future.

Case 20

One of the prime objectives of any business is survival. To stay in business a firm needs to explore the various avenues open to it. In this case the methods of working in the tool-room have been examined and newer, cheaper means are available. If such methods are not employed firms reduce their competitiveness and hence their chances of survival. The implications of such changes are that capital investment is replacing labour. A firm then has to work through how it is going to handle the problem of reducing its workforce. At Toolcraft steps were taken to minimise the impact of the reduction of the workforce in the tool-room by offering Bill Green a transfer to another department. Somehow this did not work out as intended. The work group in the tool-room was very cohesive and stuck together. The threat to remove one of their number did not meet with the group's approval and as no compromise was reached they demonstrated their feelings by walking out. In particular you should have learnt about the following:

1   change needs handling with care and skill. Many firms have gone through radical changes in recent times and this has put pressure on management to demonstrate skills of a high order in periods of transition. The skills needed are communication skills and human relations skills. Tool-craft exhibited quite an open policy on communication but still failed to hear the signals coming back;

2 acceptable alternatives need to be pursued. An offer was made to Bill Green which was not accepted. In the end the rejection led to severe consequences for the employee (redundancy) and the firm (a strike). Such an outcome will have soured relations and any changes that may be proposed in the future will probably be opposed. The firm did not seem to want to seek alternatives apart from the one put forward. Consultation involves the skill of listening. Did the firm pursue asking if any of the current tool-room workers wished to leave on early retirement?

3 redundancy is an extreme solution to the problem, especially without notice. Prior to the installation of the machine, and verifying whether the estimated savings are forthcoming, the decision to make Bill Green redundant seems extreme. Could Bill Green be kept on until the machine had been commissioned and then a solution found? Often circumstances change and a solution appears fortuitously;

4 selection for redundancy or transfer needs careful thought. The policy of the last in, first out can be a poor policy. Such an employee is likely to be young and may not wish to go and the firm is loosing out on their investment in his training. With a full working life ahead Bill Green had potentially much to offer. A policy of volunteers first has much to commend it.